# Journey:
## WALKING INTO THE HEART OF JESUS

By Linda Withers

*Claudia,*
*May your journey be full of surprises from the Lord - bringing joy and love to your heart and soul!*
*♡ Linda*

Journey: Walking into the Heart of Jesus
Copyright © Linda Withers 2019

Arrow, a Self-publishing Division
of Red Arrow Media, LLC

All rights reserved.

No part of this manuscript may be used or reproduced in any matter whatsoever without written permission from the publisher except in the case of brief quotations embodied in critical articles and reviews.

All Scripture quotations, unless otherwise indicated, are taken from The Passion Translation®. Copyright © 2017, 2018 by Passion & Fire Ministries, Inc. Used by permission. All rights reserved. ThePassionTranslation.com.

Scripture quotations marked NIV are taken from THE HOLY BIBLE, NEW INTERNATIONAL VERSION®, NIV® Copyright © 1973, 1978, 1984, 2011 by Biblica, Inc.® Used by permission. All rights reserved worldwide.

Scripture quotations marked NKJV are taken from the New King James Version®. Copyright © 1982 by Thomas Nelson. Used by permission. All rights reserved.

Scripture quotations marked MSG are taken from The Message. Copyright © 1993, 1994, 1995, 1996, 2000, 2001, 2002. Used by permission of NavPress Publishing Group.

Scripture quotations marked NLT are taken from the Holy Bible, New Living Translation, copyright © 1996, 2004, 2015 by Tyndale House Foundation. Used by permission of Tyndale House Publishers, Inc., Carol Stream, Illinois 60188. All rights reserved.

Cover & Interior Design: Amy Renée Miller
Illustrations: Karen Falconer • karenfalconerarts.com

Instagram: @redarrowmedia
Twitter: @RedArrowMedia1
Facebook: redarrowmedia
ISBN: 978-0-9965695-9-0

Printed in the United States

# TABLE OF CONTENTS

Introduction . . . . . . . . . . . . . . . . . . . . . . . . . . . . . . . . . . . 4

Chapter 1: I Am Loved . . . . . . . . . . . . . . . . . . . . . . . . . 7

Chapter 2: Before You Were Born . . . . . . . . . . . . . . . 19

Chapter 3: Tears . . . . . . . . . . . . . . . . . . . . . . . . . . . . . . 29

Chapter 4: The Mind Of Christ . . . . . . . . . . . . . . . . . . 41

Chapter 5: Glorious Perfection . . . . . . . . . . . . . . . . . . 51

Chapter 6: Wait . . . . . . . . . . . . . . . . . . . . . . . . . . . . . . . 61

Chapter 7: The Riches In Glory . . . . . . . . . . . . . . . . . . 73

Conclusion: Into Joy . . . . . . . . . . . . . . . . . . . . . . . . . . 85

# INTRODUCTION

*"In him you have been made extravagantly rich in every way. You have been endowed with a wealth of inspired utterances and the riches that come from your intimate knowledge of him. For the reality of the truth of Christ is seen among you and strengthened through your experience of him."*
*1 Corinthians 1:5–6*

———

Our beliefs are powerful. They have the power to keep us in chains or to set us free. The challenge comes in life's journey as we decide what we are going to accept as our truth. For this very reason it is of utmost importance that we set our sights on Jesus, the author and finisher of our faith, and learn to believe only what He says about us.

I have been running after Jesus most of my life, serving Him with passion and desiring for all those in my realm of influence to know and love Him. Yet with all this, I found myself feeling chained, as if I had a leash around my neck that would not quite reach the places I longed to go, the places God was calling me. Sometimes it seemed as if I were in a glass box and could see the path, but I was stuck, unable to break through the boundaries that were holding me back.

After many years of Spirit-filled ministry with beautiful people in the body of Christ, the Lord began to show me that somewhere along my life's path, I had disqualified myself from knowing His full truth. A persistent battle with unworthiness created a belief that a close rapport with God, including revelation and power, were for those who were smarter or better in some way, people who were chosen. In my mind, I had set up a fortress, believing lies that would keep me from the deep intimacy my heavenly Father desired. The restraint I felt was completely of my own making, and even though I had set my life in Him, lies deeply embedded in my heart were keeping me separated from the abundant life for which I was created. I read the truth in the Word and knew the truth in my head; however, there is a huge gap between head and heart.

Almost without my knowledge, God set me on a journey to increase my intimacy with Him. Through Scripture God invited me to ask questions. In return, He gave me precious treasure: Holy Spirit-imparted imaginations, or answers in the form of visions. I believe God uses many paths to speak to His children. In the Bible God often spoke to His people in the forms of dreams and visions. In Genesis 37 Joseph had a symbolic dream about his future. In Acts 10:13 God spoke new revelation to Peter through a vision of unclean animals. The Holy Spirit speaks to me through pictures in my mind in the form of stories, leading me to search out mysteries with the Lord. The symbolic narratives are intimate and personal in nature, challenging me to journey past the barriers I created to keep out Holy Spirit revelation. As God spoke to me through these visions, the lies in my heart began to dissolve, and His truth began to emerge. As my partnership with God widened, He gave me more visions to process, revealing His deep love and confidence in me.

Throughout my years of teaching children and adults, I find that everyone needs to hear God for themselves in order to see amazing transformation in their lives. In my current ministry of speaking and teaching, I have shared these God-given stories to create worship experiences for others during retreats and prayer meetings. People are transformed as they step into the presence of God and experience His amazing love. I decided to write this book to encourage others to journey with Jesus to new and amazing places so they can hear God for themselves and remove any barriers that might be keeping them from His abundant life.

Through this book I share these revelations and encourage you to allow Jesus to pull you into your own adventure with Him, renewing your mind and encountering Jesus. Some of us are seekers, some seers, some feelers, hearers, or knowers. No matter how you understand God, I invite you to go deeper with Him. This journey is between you and God, and He speaks to all of us in the way we can hear. He knows us personally as our Creator; therefore, He knows exactly how we hear Him. This is about building a relationship with the Father, learning to hear His voice.

Each chapter begins with a question to God, followed by the vision I received in answer. Explore God's direct answers to you through the activation questions at the end of each chapter, allowing each lesson and chapter to build on one another as you receive new revelation from God. Take as much time as you need. Whether done individually or as a small group, believe God will speak to you as you learn to hear from Him personally. Suggestions for using this material in a small group are located at the end of the book.

Step through the open door, and enjoy the journey. I believe God is calling us to come closer, shed the lies that have been holding us back, and embrace the truth that will set us free.

## CHAPTER ONE: I AM LOVED

*"I urge you, my brothers and sisters, for the sake of the name of our Lord Jesus Christ, to agree to live in unity with one another and put to rest any division that attempts to tear you apart. Be restored as one united body living in perfect harmony. Form a consistent choreography among yourselves, having a common perspective with shared values."*
*1 Corinthians 1:10*

---

We live in a world where everyone is clamoring to be heard and known, where the current tension to be right in our culture is unrestrained and often violent. I am grieved with the discord in the world, but mostly grieved with the lack of love and honor within the church and in many families. It seems we have lost the ability and desire to really know the people in our lives, causing the body of believers to divide over different opinions—parents are unable to hear and know their children; spouses have irreconcilable differences; Christians judge and criticize those who don't think exactly like they do, separating themselves into exclusive communities and denominations that do not challenge or truly edify each other. In 1 Corinthians 1:10 Paul clearly calls those who love the Lord to unity, a place of peace and wholeness. If unity is our mission, then why do churches believe so differently about what is right that they split apart? Why do families who say they love Jesus separate because of conflict? Why does unity seem impossible for the body of Christ?

When I look closely in the depths of my spirit, I find real tension around this subject. There are many absolute truths in the Word of God, so it makes sense that we would actually want to be right about those truths. If we are right, then we feel safe and secure. People with different views can often confuse us or cause us to doubt our understanding of God. But if we as Christians are called to love each other even in—or especially in—the midst of wanting to feel right, whether about our beliefs or about how we have been treated, then how do we avoid feeling fear or offense by those who hurt or offend us? How do we live in harmony and wholeness with others when we disagree? How do we learn to love well?

One Sunday morning during a sermon, my pastor challenged our church to lay down our differences and come together as one body. As he spoke, the Holy Spirit imparted a story across my mind, a picture that became clear as the story unfolded, and I knew it was treasure from heaven.

## The Story

A crowd of people was waiting to get into a banquet hall. Everyone was wearing identical coats made of a very fine, thin material that was almost invisible. On the front pocket of each coat were the words: I AM RIGHT. Before the people could enter the hall, they were asked to remove their coats, but the coats were fitted so tightly to each of their bodies that all were struggling to remove them. When it was my turn to enter, I was asked to remove my coat, although I had not been aware I was wearing one. As I looked down at my body, I saw that, yes, I too wore a coat and on the breast pocket were the same words as all the others: I AM RIGHT. I wondered, "Why would I be wearing a coat like this? Where did I get it?"

Suddenly, Jesus walked into the banquet hall, and as He passed me, He smiled as if He knew what I was thinking and beckoned me to enter. In the banquet hall were tables as far as my eye could see. I felt strangely vulnerable, almost naked without my coat, but as we sat and I began to speak with the other guests at my table, I sensed amazing peace during the conversation. I felt myself listening to what others were saying without feeling a need to recite my viewpoint. The conversation was delightful and insightful. Each person carefully listened to the other as if they were speaking of a great treasure to be found, yet we were simply talking about daily life. I felt like I knew these people deeply, and I myself felt known, yet we had all just met.

As this special evening ended, the waiters brought the coats and placed them on the tables. They all looked exactly alike, and I wondered how each person would find his or her coat. It was not long before I realized each person would have to try on many coats until he or she discovered which one fit perfectly and belonged to them. I picked up the first coat and slipped my arms into the sleeves. Immediately I felt red hot, and anger, terror, and hatred poured into my heart. This coat was inflexible and uncomfortable. It belonged to someone who had been abused and had a soul crowded with hostility due to the immense emotional pain. I quickly took it off and picked up another. The next coat felt better, but as soon as I pulled it tight, my vision saw only in black and white. I sensed the only answers in life were right and wrong, yes or no, my way or no way. This feeling frightened me because I love creativity and color and enjoy thinking outside the box. This coat was definitely not for me.

The next coat was extremely tight, and the minute I was in it I began to feel starved, ravenous for food, attention, love, and acceptance. When I looked around at the kind people at my table, I could only see people who were out to get me and steal from me. I even felt compelled to take something from the table that was not mine. I had an urgent feeling of lack. I took off that coat and continued to the next coat. With relief, the next coat let me see beautiful color everywhere. Everything I saw had a lush, beautiful hue, but although my eyes were seeing beautiful things, my heart felt deep pain. The beauty given by the owner of this coat came at a high price of deep sorrow. I took off this coat, not wanting to participate in this person's pain no matter how lovely the view. Coat after coat, sadness, judgment, criticism, jealousy, hate, and fear were attached. As I moved through the coats, I began to panic that I would never find my coat. I was so weary. Trying each coat and having a different emotion each time was more than I could handle.

Then I felt a presence beside me and looked up to see Jesus. As I looked into His eyes, I saw profound sadness. It occurred to me that this was what Jesus had taken to the cross for all of us. He endured the heavy weight of all these experiences for all of His people. I looked at Him with tears in my eyes and asked, "If You endured all of this, why are we still wearing these coats?" He smiled and pointed to the last coat on the table. I tried it on, and yes, it was mine. For a brief moment, I felt safe again. I was secure in my own little world, the good and the bad. I finally found the right coat. That good feeling only lasted a minute before I understood that others had been trying on my coat and taking on my burdens as I had theirs. Suddenly, I wanted nothing more than to shed my coat, but it wouldn't budge. No matter how hard I tried, I couldn't get it off. I cried out, "Help me, Jesus! I am sorry to have clung so tightly to this coat."

Immediately I was transported to the most beautiful place I had ever seen. I was alone, standing in front of Jesus, His beautiful eyes full of love. He drew me in, and my heart melted. As He drew me close, my coat loosened. As He continued to love on me, my coat slowly fell away, leaving me raw and vulnerable. I thought, "I can't go out like this. What will happen to me?" Then Jesus handed me a new coat—His coat. It was stunning, and I became afraid to try it on, but He helped me into the coat, and it fit perfectly. I had never felt such love. I suddenly knew who I was—I was His.

I was back in the banquet hall. Everyone was there wearing his or her own coat, but I was different. Now when I looked into everyone's eyes, I saw Jesus, and I could not help but love each and every one of them. I felt the burden of everyone's life experiences, but wearing His coat, I could love each of them and listen to them without carrying the hurt and pain of their burdens. I no longer wanted to pass my own judgment on them.

Jesus led me out of the room. As we left, more people were entering with their coats. I wanted to yell at them, "No, no, no! Take off your coats and trade them for this coat, His coat, a coat full of love and acceptance! You don't have to be right. You don't have to carry your burden. You don't have to be afraid." Jesus took my hand, and I understood that one must be ready and willing to give up his or her coat in exchange for His and that the only way to experience the peace and joy I felt was to wear His coat daily, giving up I AM RIGHT for I AM LOVED.

## The Interpretation

The beautiful story of the coats portrayed to me how so many of us are stuck in our own life experiences, believing lies that cause us to need to be right and to be offended by differences. It's simply safer that way. At first I believed it was more about the church in general, yet as I pondered the story, I knew this was God's voice speaking directly to me, answering my question about loving well. I quickly learned how difficult it really is to take off my I AM RIGHT coat, my self-made protection to keep me from the vulnerability of exposing my soul. What if, when I took off my coat, I was truly unlovable?

As strange as that sounds after a lifetime of knowing God, the question presented itself. Knowing the truth in my head that Jesus loves me is not the same as knowing it in my heart. Apparently, my insecurity had been deeply hidden, and I began to see how much of my life had been spent striving to "be" someone. I loved ministering to others and teaching truth, but I had also been stuck in my own world, carefully guarding lies that held me captive.

Jesus tells us in John 5 that if we abide in Him and allow Him to abide in us, we will bear much fruit. Abide means "to remain in, to dwell, to submit to." For me to abide in Him, I would have to go along with what He says about me in His word, to believe it, study it, and propel my faith into it, allowing me to experience this love through His power. I would need to camp in 1 Peter 2:9, which tells me that I am chosen, a royal priesthood, a holy nation, God's special possession, that I may declare the praises of Him who called me out of darkness into His wonderful light.

With this in mind, I began the challenge of taking off the self-protection I had been wearing. To do this, I would have to lay down all the experiences in my life that caused me pain—the things people had said or done to me that taught me I was unlovable—and lay them at the feet of Jesus. Either I believed He died for all of it, or I didn't. There was no middle ground. If I were going to break off the chains holding me back, I would have to sit with Jesus and allow Him to remove my coat. This would not be easy. It would mean facing my own pain. This began an unraveling process in which Jesus allowed me to see what part of Him was missing in my life, causing the stumbling blocks to fall away. Each day, I would focus on a scripture, invite Jesus to speak to me about it, and then allow the Holy Spirit to take me to a negative stronghold that needed to be broken so I could choose the truth and release the lies. It sounds simple, but in reality it took work on my part to declare over and over again what Jesus was saying about me so I could completely let go of the lies I had been believing. This is a lifelong process, but once the unraveling had begun, the voice of the Lord became clearer each day. I learned that until I truly believed Jesus perfectly loves me, it would be impossible for me to love others. I would always be afraid of their disapproval, of what they could take away from me, or of how they might hurt or disappoint me.

In the story, I had the opportunity to put on different coats and step into other people's belief systems. It was daunting and difficult to endure. In reality, living other people's life experiences and fully seeing from their points of view is not only impossible, it's also unnecessary. Only the deep love of Christ will allow me to see past a person's beliefs and expressions of pain and into his or her heart. God's answer to my question, "How do we live in unity?" was simple. I do not have to agree with another's opinion, choices, or even what they do to me. I only have to love. By knowing I was loved regardless of being right, that it was not God's command that I "convince others well," there was no longer any reason for offense. I could see who others were created to be and, through the overflowing of God's love, see how much they too are loved by Jesus.

The activations that follow are some of the steps through which I journeyed to begin putting on Jesus's beautiful coat of love. The truth of I AM LOVED needed to seep into the darkest corners of my soul, empowering me to love God and others well and to answer the call of a desperate world to be loved and celebrated.

## Activations

In order to process the activations in each chapter, I encourage you to choose a creative path that allows you to express what you hear from the Lord. You may want to try something new, as the purpose of these activations is to allow you to hear from God for yourself from your heart in a new way. Just as God has made each person different with unique skills, talents, abilities, and ways of hearing from Him, so has He given each of us ways of expressing His words to us. This may include writing, painting, music, photography, numbers, words, art, or any other expression you love, even simply writing thoughts in your journal. Invite the Holy Spirit into your time, asking Him to open your spiritual ears to hear what the Father is saying to you, remembering that He speaks only of His love for you. Jesus already took care of our sin, therefore there will be no condemnation from the Father. He is always speaking over us what He knows to be true about our genuine identity.

There are three activations. Read through them and then start where you feel the most led. Take your time. Allow the things that minister to your soul to become a lifestyle, giving you access to the mind of Christ.

## *Activation 1: I Am Right*

- Ask God to remind you of times earlier this week when you believed "I am right and you are wrong," or when you were angry, offended, or hurt by another person. Write these down along with a short statement of why you were right. It is not necessary to change your opinion, but to find out why you believe what you do.

- Sit with your list and consider other emotions that may be connected to each experience. For example, perhaps getting upset when someone cut you off in traffic this morning reminded you of feeling taken advantage of or being insignificant. Maybe your boss's disappointment stirred up negative thoughts of inadequacy. Write the emotions and thoughts connected to your experiences.

- Ask God to show you other life experiences that formed your I AM RIGHT ideas. Was it important to agree with your parents, or did you face punishment if you didn't? Were you only heard in your family when you disagreed? What life experiences stand out in regard to the emotions you described earlier? Ask God for the grace to submit those experiences and feelings to Jesus. Remember, He died for all of them in exchange for His peace and joy in your life.

- In the story, the coat is a symbol of our emotions, actions, and feelings that we live with daily, along with the reasons behind what we feel and how we respond. Use your chosen creative path to design your own coat. This is only to help you step back and look at your life, learning about the why behind what you think and do. What color is your coat? What fabric is it made of? How does it feel when you have it on—is it loose, tight, thin, uncomfortable?

- Describe what someone else would feel and see if they put on your coat (your life experiences and reactions to them).

- Ask the Lord to show you areas in your life or specific memories where you might need to be forgiven and areas where you might need to forgive. Allow the Holy Spirit to help you remove this part of your coat by surrendering each area to Him. For each situation revealed to you, write out a statement of repentance or forgiveness.

## *Activation 2: I Am Loved*

In my vision, the only way to experience love for others was to wear Jesus's coat daily and to give up I AM RIGHT for I AM LOVED. If I kept His coat on and my eyes on Him, then my life experiences would be renewed by Jesus and I would be able to listen to and empathize with others—even those whose lives I disagreed with or didn't understand.

- Find 2-3 Bible verses that tell you what Jesus thinks about you and write them down. Begin every day this week by reading these verses, reminding yourself that no matter what happens today, no matter what others say or do, these words are the truth about who you are.

- Ask Jesus to tell you how He sees you. Write down words you "hear" about yourself. These may come as words, pictures, song lyrics, etc. If you struggle with this, ask the Holy Spirit to help you receive God's love. Trusting that He will, keep coming back to this step each day until you are able to hear and receive His amazing unconditional love for you.

- Read 1 John 4:11-13:
  "Delightfully loved ones, if he loved us with such tremendous love, then 'loving one another' should be our way of life! No one has ever gazed upon the fullness of God's splendor. But if we love one another, God makes his permanent home in us, and we make our permanent home in him, and his love is brought to its full expression in us. And he has given us his Spirit within us so that we can have the assurance that he lives in us and that we live in him."

- Rewrite these verses in your own words, describing what it is like to wear Jesus's coat of love.

- Read Jesus's prayer to the Father for you in John 17:21-24:
  "I pray for them all to be joined together as one even as you and I, Father, are joined together as one. I pray for them to become one with us so that the world will recognize that you sent me. For the very glory you have given to me I have given them so that they will be joined together as one and experience the same unity that we enjoy. You live fully in me and now I live fully in them so that they will experience perfect unity, and the world will be convinced that you have sent me, for they will see that you love each one of them with the same passionate love that you have for me. Father, I ask that you allow everyone that you have given to me to be with me where I am! Then they will see my full glory—the very splendor you have placed upon me because you have loved me even before the beginning of time."

- Write out 1-2 steps that you will take daily to begin abiding in God's love. For example, memorizing or reciting a passage of Scripture of God's love every morning, or at the end of your day writing a note of thanksgiving for every place you experienced God's love throughout your day. Note the places you possibly failed to give love to others, yet remember, there is no condemnation given to you, only love and encouragement for the next day.

- Use a creative path to describe what I AM LOVED means in your life. How would this coat feel or look? Describe how your daily life would be different if this were truly the way you approached your family, friends, coworkers, or even strangers.

- Write out or share aloud a prayer to Jesus thanking Him for His love and the treasure He has deposited in all His children.

## *Activation 3: Unity through Understanding*

- Read Colossians 3:12-14, and discuss or write down what it means to you:
"You are always and dearly loved by God! So robe yourself with virtues of, since you have been divinely chosen to be holy. Be merciful as you endeavor to understand others, and be compassionate, showing kindness toward all. Be gentle and humble, unoffendable in your patience with others. Tolerate the weaknesses of those in the family of faith, forgiving one another in the same way you have been graciously forgiven by Jesus Christ. If you find fault with someone, release this same gift of forgiveness to them. For love is supreme and must flow through each of these virtues. Love becomes the mark of true maturity."

- Think about one person in your life with whom you strongly disagree or consider your "enemy." Now imagine that you are putting on his or her coat. What does it feel like? What are the first things that come to your mind when you put on the coat? Ask the Holy Spirit to show you how that person views life and why.

- Now ask the Holy Spirit to show you what Jesus thinks about this person. What treasure is in this person that you cannot see? Write out a short sentence about this person's coat and how it might be covering the treasure in his or her heart. If you get blocked, you may have to take a break until you can hear from God.

- Ask God to show you how He views this person, to give you eyes to see the treasure in him or her. Write out a short sentence that begins, "When Jesus looks at [insert person's name], He sees . . ."

- For some of you, this person has truly hurt you through abuse or abandonment, falsely accusing you of wrongdoing, or stealing something or someone from you. There are few relationships where forgiveness isn't needed, but this will be impossible without the love and grace of God at work in your life. Ask God to lead you to a place where you can forgive, or if that seems too difficult, to help you get to the point where you want to forgive.

- Finish with a prayer for your heart to soften in understanding as you view this person.

> *"I understood that one must be ready and willing to give up his or her coat in exchange for His and that the only way to experience the peace and joy I felt was to wear His coat daily, giving up I AM RIGHT for I AM LOVED."*

## CHAPTER TWO: BEFORE YOU WERE BORN

*"Before I formed you in the womb I knew you."*
Jeremiah 1:5 NIV

---

I love gifts, both giving and receiving. A perfect gift is personal and says, "I know you, I am thinking about you, and you are loved and valuable." I sought to give such a gift to my friend for her birthday—something imaginative, a gift that would connect to her heart and trigger celebration and significance within. While considering different items I could get her, I realized that a purchased gift did not have the impact I desired, so I sought the Holy Spirit for inspiration. I closed my eyes and asked the Holy Spirit to show me what Jesus sees in her. I was hoping for a list of words or a symbolic picture, yet He gave me a story, one that illustrated God's extravagant love for my friend.

After receiving the vision, incredible joy and wonder filled my heart. I designed a beautiful box covered with angel wings to present to her with the letter inside. Yet in all my excitement to share, I felt the Lord tugging at my heart. I stopped to listen, then heard His familiar voice say, "Write the story for yourself." Immediately my heart said, "No, thank you." I pondered why I would not want to hear a story of God's great love such as this for myself. Why was I not just as excited about my story as I was about hers? I slowly began to understand that this was another step in my journey with Him. God had already begun to show me that learning to love well would mean I must love myself, but lies still existed in the corners of my soul, keeping me from the remarkable truth of the Father's love for me. I sat down to write the story for myself—but nothing came. I knew I could simply give my gift to my friend and move on, or I could listen to the still, small voice of the Lord and allow myself to wander beyond the closed doors of my soul yet again . . .

## The Story

As written for my friend:

Before you were born, I saw you walking with Jesus. There was laughter and great joy between the two of you. Hand and hand, He led you through a beautiful, commanding gate into a room marked: "The Riches of Glory for the Saints." I watched angels look on with pleasure and delight as if you were about to take on an assignment of insurmountable purpose.

He led you through the gate, and somehow I knew your soul had been chosen to live among those made in His glorious image. As you stepped into the beautiful, deep, blue river, your eyes were mesmerized by the dazzling and intense color coming from the diamonds, sapphires, and emeralds covering the riverbed. Jesus bent down and pulled the color out of the water, splashing it into your eyes. Your eyes beamed a brilliant blue, and at once I could see Him, His image, in your eyes. He took a handful of diamonds, kissed them, and placed them in your hands. Then, covering your hands with His, He touched your heart. The diamonds disappeared as His perfect treasure became part of you.

As you continued down the river, the angels were singing, harps were playing, and the most beautiful music one could hear rang in the air. The angels began singing over you, and soon you were singing with them. He had given you the voice of angels to take to earth. The two of you traveled together, stopping along the way as He lavished gifts on you, preparing for your birth.

There were many gifts along the path, yet Jesus only picked up the ones that had your name on them. I saw a box bearing His name, translucent and multicolored like a rainbow with birds flying all around. He handed it to you, and when you opened it, magnificent and lovely things began to swirl around you. His very own gift of creating beauty was handed to you. As you closed the box, you noticed your name alongside His. One of your assignments would be to bring His beauty to the earth through your own creations.

In an instant, the two of you began to laugh because the next gift was so odd and amusing, full of bright colors and silly shapes creating the happy, joyful spirit in you. His laughter, His joy, were to be yours to share with the world where He was sending you. At one point along the path, He gave you a sword, one of great authority for spiritual warfare. You would be strong and courageous—two qualities that would be necessary for your earthly assignment.

There was a turn in the river, and just beyond the path was the most majestic mountain made of pure gold. You and Jesus sat down together by the side of the mountain. He placed His hand on His heart, then as He opened His hand to you, a river of gold ran right into your own heart. For the first time, He spoke: "Your heart is made with gold from Mine, for you are made in My image." I knew He had just given you His love, a love that would be there to conquer your fear and bring His unconditional love to the world.

At once, you came to a door, the biggest, most exquisite door I have ever seen. Angels opened the door, ushering you into the throne room. The highest seats belonged to Jesus and His Father. Everywhere, angels were singing praises to the King. There at the throne of God, you experienced something that would be placed in your heart forever: Father God opened His arms, and you ran to Him. When you jumped into His arms, His love enveloped your very soul. You came alive and saw in His face the joy and delight of you—His creation, His child, His daughter.

In His lap He had two boxes tied with ribbons of gold. The first box contained a rolled-up scroll that read: "Your destiny." Father God opened it and read it aloud. The sound of His voice was deafening yet loving; one would know in an instant that creation was taking place. Your life's purpose was set. The second box had the words "Your will" inscribed on it. He handled this box with great care, as if it were the most important thing in all of the kingdom to Him. There was a lock on the box, and as He handed you the box, He also handed you the key. The law of the kingdom of love required that God could never touch this box—whether you opened it or left it closed, it would all be up to you. You laughed at the thought that you would choose anything but the destiny laid out for you or the incredible love you experienced with the Father. He grew serious for only a second, knowing the task of surrendering your will would not be as easy as you thought. When you unlocked the box, you found another bejeweled key that read: "The blood of the Lamb." This would be the key to unlocking your destiny and to surrendering your will . . . and you had it in your hand.

Those moments with the father slowly faded, becoming more and more dreamlike, until in an instant you found yourself listening to a heartbeat—your own. For the moment, you were comfortably growing inside your mother's womb. On the day of your birth, I saw the face of Jesus. His joy was overflowing; His eyes rejoiced. There would be nothing you could ever do to erase the love He had for you.

## The Interpretation

For days, I read the story over and over, enjoying the thought of intimately knowing my heavenly Father. I honestly believed He knew me before I was born and that I was created in His love. I was His marvelous creation. Nevertheless, the words "it would all be up to you" haunted me. Had I gotten that part of the story wrong? Was it possible that I would not get it right, not be good enough, not make the right choices? My heart was challenging what I knew in my head.

"The blood of the Lamb" then echoed in my mind. I began to focus on the sacrifice of my Savior. Because I am visual, I imagined His death on the cross. I forced myself to look into His eyes, and after a while, my heart melted into a puddle of love and thanksgiving. It is simply impossible to camp at the cross very long and not be overwhelmed by His amazing sacrificial love. There is no greater offering. Hebrews 12:2 NKJV says, "Looking unto Jesus, the author and finisher of our faith, who for the joy that was set before Him endured the cross." Allowing me open access to intimacy with my heavenly Father was the "joy set before him." I am His true joy.

Just as in the story, the key was in my hand, but what would I do with it? I chose to go forward, seeking the Father's heart residing in me. The following activations are some of the steps the Lord took me through to pull out my own treasure and to help me more deeply believe that I am known by Him, significant, and loved.

This story was intended for my friend and for me, but this is also a story about you. The Father's gifts reside within you. Wealth and riches of the heart are yours to search. Read the story again, this time as God's thoughts about you. Then work through the activations, allowing yourself to reflect on the immense, marvelous treasure carried only by you. The treasures of God in you are your inheritance. You hold the key.

## Activations

There are three activations. Read through them and then start where you feel the most led. Take your time. Allow the things that minister to your soul to become a lifestyle, giving you access to the mind of Christ.

### *Activation 1: Before You Were Born*

- Read Psalm 139:13–18:
  "You formed my innermost being, shaping my delicate inside and my intricate outside, and wove them all together in my mother's womb. I thank you, God, for making me so mysteriously complex! Everything you do is marvelously breathtaking. It simply amazes me to think about it! How thoroughly you know me, Lord! You even formed every bone in my body when you created me in the secret place, carefully, skillfully shaping me from nothing to something. You saw who you created me to be before I became me! Before I'd ever seen the light of day, the number of days you planned for me were all recorded in your book. Every single moment you are thinking of me! How precious and wonderful to consider that you cherish me constantly in your every thought! O God, your desires toward me are more than the grains of sand on every shore! When I awake each morning, you're still with me."

- Choose a creative path (painting, journaling, discussing) in which to express what this passage of Scripture means to you and about you. Rewrite it in your own words.

- Make a list of the things that bring life and joy to you (being in nature, cooking, writing, etc.). Add to your list the gifts, talents, or personality traits God has blessed you with. How are these important for and related to you purpose in life? (For instance, your love of painting may be a way for you to connect to God and to display God's beauty and creativity to others.)

- Is there any passion or dream for your life that you have disqualified yourself from? If so, ask God what He thinks about this and write down the first thing that comes to your mind.

- Craft your own "Before I was born" story by prayerfully considering and completing the following statements:

    "Before I was born, God planned for me to . . ."

    "God created me to enjoy . . ."

    "God loves when I . . ."

    "God's treasure in me is . . ."

    "I am here on earth to . . ."

## Activation 2: The Throne Room

- Read each verse below and allow the Holy Spirit to speak to you about the Father's love for you. Highlight the verses that connect with your heart, and note the ones that may not feel true to you.

    "Look at the birds of the air; they do not sow or reap or store away in barns, and yet your heavenly Father feeds them. Are you not much more valuable than they?" (Matthew 6:26 NIV)

    "If you, then, though you are evil, know how to give good gifts to your children, how much more will your Father in heaven give good gifts to those who ask him!" (Matthew 7:11 NIV)

    "The Spirit you received does not make you slaves, so that you live in fear again; rather, the Spirit you received brought about your adoption to sonship. And by him we cry, 'Abba, Father.'" (Romans 8:15 NIV)

    "I will be a Father to you, and you will be my sons and daughters, says the Lord Almighty." (2 Corinthians 6:18 NIV and 2 Samuel 7:14 NIV)

"Praise be to the God and Father of our Lord Jesus Christ, who has blessed us in the heavenly realms with every spiritual blessing in Christ.  For he chose us . . . . In love he predestined us for adoption to sonship through Jesus Christ." (Ephesians 1:3–5 NIV)

"Now to [the Father] who is able to do immeasurably more than all we ask or imagine, according to his power that is at work within us, to him be glory in the church and in Christ Jesus throughout all generations, for ever and ever! Amen." (Ephesians 3:20–21 NIV)

"See what great love the Father has lavished on us, that we should be called children of God!" (1 John 3:1 NIV)

- Imagine you are entering (and welcome in) the throne room of God. Use your chosen creative path to describe the throne room. What does it look like? How do you feel there? What is God doing or saying?

- Visualize talking to God on His throne, thanking Him for the truths found in the above Scripture verses. Bring before Him the ones that are true but don't feel true in your life.

- Choose one verse above and write out a statement of faith. For example: "My heavenly Father is able to do immeasurably more than I ask or imagine. He invites me into His loving arms, challenging me to ask Him for this."

## Activation 3: The Key

"For God so loved the world, that he gave his only begotten Son, that whosoever believeth in him should not perish, but have everlasting life."  (John 3:16 KJV)

- Imagine two boxes: one holds your destiny and the other holds your will. Look at the box holding your will. Imagine that you hold the key, the key that was given to you only by the blood of the Lamb. Is there something holding you back from complete surrender to God? Write this down.

- Read Revelation 12:7–12. Write down or say aloud: "The accuser has been defeated by the blood of the Lamb. You have been set free to receive God's perfect love." Rewrite this verse in your own words, ending with a statement declaring who you are in God's eyes.

*"For the moment, you were comfortably growing inside your mother's womb. On the day of your birth, I saw the face of Jesus. His joy was overflowing; His eyes rejoiced. There would be nothing you could ever do to erase the love He had for you."*

## CHAPTER THREE: TEARS

*"You've kept track of all my wandering and my weeping. You've stored my many tears in your bottle—not one will be lost. You care about me every time I've cried. For they are all recorded in your book of remembrance."*
Psalm 56:8

---

Running from pain and suffering is almost required in a culture that demands pleasure at any cost. We find ways to numb ourselves, shutting down our emotions in order to live pain free. Passing this behavior to the next generation, many parents go to extremes to make sure their children don't experience pain, causing anxiety and sometimes hopelessness when pain inevitably shows up. The pain is real, yet our Savior has promised to carry it for us—but what keeps us from running to Him?

I am no different from the world: my greatest temptation is to run from pain. The inability to embrace pain, learn from it, and grow has left me limping in life. Even as a child, watching others suffer seemed to envelope my soul, for I unknowingly allowed myself to step into their pain. I quietly assumed the role of peacekeeping, which grew into rescuing as an adult. Over the years, watching my children struggle knocked the wind out of my sails; therefore, rescuing them from pain turned into a badge of honor. Pain and suffering did not fit inside my "faith" box.

My God is good; I know He is. He delivered me from my sin and lavishly loves me. Although I knew theological answers about authority and free will and what the Bible says about evil and love being a choice, I never allowed myself to lean into the familiar question: How could a good God allow so much evil? I believe we are given the key to overcome evil by the power of the Holy Spirit; however, a good God and suffering still don't seem to mesh in my worldview. Tucking them away into two different boxes seemed to work just fine for me. I carefully stuffed my pain, unanswered prayers, and struggles into a strongbox inside my soul, praying for rescue when new pain occurred.

One such time happened when my older sister suffered a brain aneurysm, leaving her with serious brain damage and causing physical problems and short-term memory loss. Her life as a wife, mother, teacher, and artist instantly transformed into one that required twenty-four-hour care. Her next fifteen years were spent daily at an extraordinary community called Brookwood, which provides meaning and purpose to adults with disabilities. She was able to shine as an artist as she painted beautiful pottery during the day and went home to be cared for by her loyal, loving husband at night. Not until she died did I realize that my desire for her perfect healing, which I prayed for daily, was the only answer acceptable to me, a mindset that caused me to miss the beautiful, powerful things God was doing in her life and family. I could only see pain and suffering (which was there), and at the same time, I rejected that pain and never allowed myself to embrace it (or feel it fully). I boxed up the pain and sought for rescue, only blinding myself to the loving, tender heart of the Father.

A few years before her death, the twenty-year-old son of my close friend was killed. There was no ability to rescue, no fix possible. Something horrible had happened. This kind of pain and suffering for my friend left me empty, as if I had fallen into a deep, dark box with no way out. I could not deliver my friend, and when my son asked me how a good God could allow this, I simply said, "God is good." It was easier to tuck this away like I had with my sister than to face it head on. Holding on to a life's worth of trouble and pain was taking its toll on my body, soul, and spirit, yet I was blind to see my mistake.

On the fifth anniversary of the death of my friend's son, I asked the Lord for a word to give her, something that would be an encouragement, for I had nothing to give. What He gave me was deeply personal, so much so that at first, I did not want to share it with anyone else but her alone. It felt like deep treasure, and indeed it turned out to be just that.

## The Story

I saw your tears; I felt my own; I fell to my knees. Why, Lord? Why so much suffering? Who will carry all this pain?

In an instant, I was swept away to a place, a weighty place so beautiful that words alone are insufficient. I stepped into a secret place where the most magnificent beings lined the room in majesty. As far as the eye could see, these beautiful beings each held a bottle. Was it a bottle of light? Of gold? Of glory? I could not tell.

No one spoke as I knelt, trembling in fear. Looking up, one bottle caught my eye, for it shone like the stars of heaven. The angel holding the bottle summoned me, and as I came near, its color stunned me: iridescent blue mixed with a majestic purple unlike any other color ever seen. I could not take my eyes off such a spectacular sight; my eyes were fixed, almost frozen, as I looked upon this jar of beauty. What did such a container possess? It could only be something worth more than all the wealth of the nations or all the hearts of men. What could it be?

As I gazed upon this bottle, I saw a name written on it—your name. The angel tipped the bottle and summoned me to look in. I trembled, looking away, but I could not hold back. The treasure within consumed me.

As I looked, I saw you, crying, brokenhearted, with tears unstoppable. Before I could reach out to you, I noticed your tears dropping into the beautiful bottle. Yes, every tear spilled into this jar, not one to be lost. As I watched the scene before me, your tears turned into gems, diamonds, and sapphires, each becoming a splash of beauty as it fell into the jar, carefully contained so as not to be lost.

I looked up at the angel as if to ask why, but then I saw beyond the tears. A great and glorious ocean, iridescent blue and majestic purple, splashing upon a beach, appeared within the jar. Each tear fell into the ocean, forming a beautiful gemstone creating the sand.

Then I saw Him, my Jesus, His eyes the color of the ocean, His smile so joyful my heart could barely contain the magnificence. I saw Him running and laughing in the sand as He was playing with someone . . . a family. I looked—it was your family. You were together, all of you, your faces happy and joyful, filled with a peace I have never seen. I watched Jesus carefully run His hand through the sand, causing joy to arise from the gems that had been your tears. Yes, the joy was coming from the gems, the diamonds and sapphires that had formerly been your tears. How could this be, such agony turned to joy? I looked again and saw you all crying yet dancing together in the sand simultaneously. Could this be? Two worlds so carefully knit together: one of pain and one of joy?

Then I asked, "Why, Lord, are these tears so important to You that none are to be lost?" Immediately the angel tipped the jar so I could no longer see the contents, but before me sat another bottle. This one was gold, so bright I could barely look upon it, but in a fleeting moment the name appeared: THE BLOOD OF THE LAMB.

I fell to the floor with my face down for fear I would die at such a precious sight. My Savior's blood, the very blood that was shed for my life. And then I understood: His blood that came from such a great sacrifice was shed for our tears—your tears, my tears, all the pain of this world. Those tears were worth more than I could think or imagine, and none were to be lost.

In an instant, I was back on my knees, tears streaming down my face . . . tears for you. Then the Lord showed me another bottle. This one had my name on it and collected my tears, the same tears He gave His life for.

At that moment, I let go, I surrendered my tears to Him who promised to carry my sadness, my pain, my heartbreak. I knew my tears would be in a safe place until heaven and earth are one. I do not understand, but I will trust.

I pray that you will allow your tears to flow freely, for not one is ever lost or wasted.

## The Interpretation

After sending the story to my friend, the Holy Spirit began to challenge me to press in to the story myself as well as share it with others. At first, I was indignant. This story was personal, deeply personal.

My heart began to soften while rereading the story, making it clear to me that this was part of my journey also. He was calling me to process my own pain. I could choose to send the story away, assuring myself it was for others, or I could open up the box in my heart that held tight to my own pain secured in my heart.

I recently read Bill Johnson's book *God is Good*. At first it was easy to read, for I know God is good. After all, if He were not, everything I believe would be false. As I began working through the corresponding study, I found my "good God" belief beginning to falter. I knew this was an invitation from God to go deeper.

I took His lead, looking at the story once again, taking on the task of opening up the strongbox of pain and unanswered questions stored deep in my soul. Something akin to soured milk lost in the dregs of the refrigerator—things like anger, hopelessness, anxiety, and fear were oozing out the edges. What was I to do with this mess?

Once again, I read through the vision, allowing the beauty of it to take hold of my heart. If I were an artist, I might be able to share it better, because there are not enough words to describe the glory I saw and the joy I felt as the scenes flashed in my mind, bringing me courage as I began to face my pain. However, it wasn't until I pressed into the picture of the blood of my Jesus that my heart let go, His immeasurable love for me won. I simply couldn't take it in. The thought that my tears are treasure to Him caused me to draw into a secret place I had never been with Him. It was there that I was able to open my lockbox, the tightly guarded container. I saw the harboring of all I do not understand growing into a pile of wreckage, the food for the depression I battled. I went to the secret place over and over, opening the box as He revealed suppressed pain. My free-flowing tears began to set me free.

As I processed each trial, I tried to see God's redeeming hand. Sometimes I could; other times I could not, yet my heart began to trust and distinctly grieve what had been lost or stolen. God was setting me free to live an abundant life. Free to trust, free to love, free to know Him.

At a Catholic funeral recently, I was challenged to see the difference between problems and mystery. The priest told us that problems, like math, are meant to be solved, yet we must lean into mystery and embrace it. I had been trying to solve mysteries, to get answers to life's most difficult questions. While my vision did not give me answers to the mystery of pain and suffering, it did set me free to release my pain and to allow the joy of the Lord to be my strength.

As for my friend, the beauty of Jesus running with her family led me to understand that Jesus would take care of her and all those I love; I simply would have to trust Him. I was never meant to carry anyone's pain or rescue them. There is no answer to such pain on this side of heaven, but I can trust the One who knows to care for my people.

I would love to tell you that now I am free to not fear pain and suffering and that I look to embrace it, but that would not be true. When people get sick, I grieve. When people suffer, I cry. Still, I am learning to go into the secret place daily, releasing my tears to Jesus. In return, joy is returning, the joy that comes from Jesus and Him alone. This joy is what gives me strength to keep fighting through the difficulties and struggles in my own life.

The following activations are steps I have learned to work through often. This is not just a one-time breakthrough. When I feel depression, sadness, or fear rearing their ugly heads, I go to my secret place with the Lord and work through the process of surrendering my pain. When my sadness is justified and even excruciating, I know there is a place I can take it, believing He will walk me through if I will trust Him. Of all the chapters in this book, this has been the most difficult, one I will surely be walking out the rest of my life. I am thankful for a fresh start, and my body and soul are relieved to get rid of the strongbox that was destroying me.

## Activations

There are three activations. Read through them and then start where you feel the most led. Because of the nature of these activations, you may need to set aside a decent amount of time so you are free to release your emotions. Find a place where you are alone. Invite the Holy Spirit to be present. Wait for Him.

### *Activation 1: Tears*

- Read Psalm 56:8: "You've kept track of all my wandering and my weeping. You've stored my many tears in your bottle—not one will be lost. For they are all recorded in your book of remembrance."

- Bring to mind a current or past pain. Sit quietly and listen to your heart. If tears come, let them flow freely, knowing they are safely cared for by Jesus. If tears don't come easily, ask the Lord to help you release your pain to Him in a way you are able.

- Now imagine a beautiful bottle or container in front of you. Ask Jesus, "Why are my tears so important to you?" Then ask Him to show you what is in your bottle of tears. Using your chosen creative path, describe what answers He gives you, what you hear or see.

- Ask the Holy Spirit to help you surrender your pain from this situation, remembering what He told you about the importance of every tear.

- Do something tangible to help you turn over your pain: write a letter to God telling Him all you feel, being very honest—He can take it. Paint of picture of your pain (colors, words, symbols) being placed in the hands of God. Take a photograph, and place it before God in your prayer time; write a song that symbolizes your pain, then sing it to Him; simply write one word or phrase, then tear it up, believing God will care for it. Go for a run, imagining your sweat is releasing pain.

- Once again, leave your tears, questions, anger, fear, etc., with Jesus and your bottle by simply writing down a few sentences declaring your desire to release these things to Him. If you struggle with this step, remember that He is patient and will help you when the right time comes.

- This week do something for someone else you know who is in pain—a short note of love, a card, a text, a phone call just to say hi.

## Activation 2: Two Worlds

- "For as the sky soars high above earth, so the way I work surpasses the way you work, and the way I think is beyond the way you think." (Isaiah 55:8-11 MSG)

- Think about the way you see a painful situation in your life and then imagine the flip side of it. What good could come from this loss, pain, or discomfort in your life? Allow Jesus to show you how to find joy in your pain, both at the same time. This may be difficult and something to be done over time. If you can't see the good, just drop it and ask the Lord to reveal something to you when you are ready. Sometimes the good is easy to discover, and sometimes there seems to be no good side at all. In these cases in my life, I simply have to trust the Lord with His promises. Examples of seeing the good from the bad in my life:

**Deep loss:** This can deepen my intimacy with God, who suffered the loss of His son, and give me more insight about who He really is. Loss also allows me to minister with authority to those experiencing loss.

**Failure:** This gives me a chance to be redeemed and empowered the next time around. Failure can bring about growth in my own life and give me authority to help others in their failure.

**Relationship problems/betrayal:** This also allows for character growth and gives me the chance to partner with Christ in His deep love for all my security.

**Anxiety:** This can be a doorway to peace, teaching me how to overcome and giving me a chance to learn about the character of God as provider.

**Depression:** This can give me the opportunity to live in the joy of the Lord.

- If you are able to find one "flip side" to your pain, then focus on the good thing for the rest of your time today. Thank God in advance for this coming to pass in your life and for the strength He will give you to walk it out.

## Activation 3: The Blood of the Lamb

- Read 1 Peter 1:17-19:
"Since you call on him as your heavenly Father, the impartial Judge who judges according to each one's works, live each day with holy awe and reverence throughout your time on earth. For you know that your lives were ransomed once and for all from the empty and futile way of life handed down from generation to generation. It was not a ransom payment of silver and gold, which eventually perishes, but the precious blood of Christ—who like a spotless, unblemished lamb was sacrificed for us."

- Take time to worship: play a favorite worship song, sing your own song to Him, or simply speak or write thanksgiving to God.

- Present yourself to God (Romans 12:1), meditating on the blood of the Lamb, the holy sacrifice that was made for you. In our daily lives, it is possible for the magnitude of the price Jesus paid for us to be overlooked, causing us not to understand God's immense love for us. As you sit in His presence, write down everything that comes to mind about the blood of the Lamb shed for you. "For you know that your lives were ransomed once and for all from the empty and futile way of life."

- Write down what it means to live each day with "holy awe and reverence throughout your time on earth."

- It is the blood of the Lamb that gives us access into the kingdom of God, a superior kingdom to ours. It is the very blood of Jesus that allows us to see life from His perspective and then actually partner with Him to bring the superior kingdom to earth.

- As you focus on the sacrifice of Jesus and your ability to step into the higher kingdom because of it, how might this bring comfort to you in the areas of pain and struggle in your life?

- Ask the Holy Spirit to show you who He is in your relationship concerning a current struggle. Sit quietly until you hear Him speak. Write down what He says to you.

- Write down what you will do with this word.

- Ask the Lord to give you a vision of something beautiful in your life now or in the future. Using your creative path, express this as a way of thanking Jesus for His precious blood.

*"Then I saw Him, my Jesus, His eyes the color of the ocean, His smile so joyful my heart could barely contain the magnificence. I saw Him running and laughing in the sand as He was playing with someone . . . a family. I looked; it was your family."*

## CHAPTER FOUR: THE MIND OF CHRIST

*"Spirit can be known only by spirit—God's Spirit and our spirits in open communion. Spiritually alive, we have access to everything God's Spirit is doing, and can't be judged by unspiritual critics. Isaiah's question, 'Is there anyone around who knows God's Spirit, anyone who knows what he is doing?' has been answered: Christ knows, and we have Christ's Spirit."*
1 Corinthians 2:14–16 MSG

---

Our response to trials in life are quick to reveal our internal structure, giving us an opportunity to build up the broken places in our lives that are keeping us from kingdom living. One such time in my life occurred while stressing over finances. My intimacy with Jesus had become distant, causing me to focus on the natural, and I could not see an answer to a current problem or a way out. My internal system was broken, for I simply had forgotten about God's provision in my life up to this point. The bridge that connects me to heaven, Jesus, had become a rescuer to whom I was simply begging for help. One night as my husband and I prayed, my panic triggered this bedtime prayer: "Lord, I need an answer tonight for this problem." I wasn't sure if this was a legal prayer, but I was stuck and needed help. I don't often get immediate answers, but this night God's answer came in the form of a dream. In the dream, I was riding a horse (I am terrified of horses) through the woods, when all of a sudden a giant two-by-four slung out in front of me, whacking me dead-center on my forehead. Just as I woke up in a horrible startle, I heard, "Change the way you think." I knew this was the answer to my question even if it wasn't the one I wanted or understood.

Romans 12:1-2 came to mind and I began the journey of renewing my mind, but changing the way I thought would take work. I needed to excavate the old before establishing the new. I evidently had been "imitating the ideals and opinions of the culture around me," not being "inwardly transformed by the Holy Spirit." I began to surrender yet again, this time on a daily basis. Reading 1 Corinthians 2, I was quickly reminded that I have access to everything God's Spirit is doing and that the mind of Christ is mine. I simply asked, "Lord, what does it look like to have the mind of Christ, and how do I access it?" I closed my eyes, and He spoke to me through a succession of memories. I knew this was the Holy Spirit, for I would never have chosen to go back into these memories.

## The Story

The first scene I saw was surprising: my fifth-grade self sitting in a small elementary school chair, looking at a Social Studies test full of questions about dates and names that I could not remember. It was a familiar and troublesome scene, and I felt the anxiety of my ten-year-old self struggling to the point of tears to perform well on the test. I looked at my test, and as a tear splashed on my paper, I saw the word STUPID written across it in dark red ink. "Why, Lord, would you bring me here?" I wondered. This was an awful and forgotten memory, yet somehow I felt a strange peace as I progressed further into the memory . . . there was more to it than I knew. Jesus handed me a pair of lavender sunglasses to put on, changing the view of the memory completely. I saw Jesus there with me in the classroom, and like a loving father would, He put me in His lap, comforting my fear. I glanced at the failed test on my desk to see the word SMART written across the page—the word STUPID all but vanished. The renewed vision transformed this memory in an instant, removing the pain of a little girl and dismantling the lie from my heart.

Jesus took my hand, and we walked into another forgotten memory. I saw myself sinking quickly to the bottom of a swimming pool as a very young child and saw FEAR written on the bottom of the pool in giant black letters. Strangely enough, as I watched the memory unfold, I did not feel fear, but just as before, felt peace. Putting on the lavender sunglasses, I saw Jesus right there pulling me out of the water. I watched as we walked across the top of the water with no effort at all, hand in hand. The look on my face was joyful, for the word LOVE formed across the ripples. Arriving on dry ground, Jesus picked me up and hugged me as if He would never let go. Once again, this transformed memory brought change to my soul; a knowing that Jesus was always with me filled my heart.

The vision changed as Jesus took my hand again and walked me into the backyard of my childhood home where I was swimming with friends. Instead of joy and laughter, I saw a deep sadness on my face in this memory, knowing immediately it was the day I learned of my parents' divorce. I saw the word ABANDONED, reminding me of this moment deeply set in my soul. Jesus handed me the lavender sunglasses, and I put them on over the hot tears running down my face, for once again, this was not a place I wanted to experience. Immediately the scene changed, and I saw my child-self standing in front of a large, commanding door. I watched the scene only to see the most wonderful sight: my heavenly Father with His arms stretched wide, inviting me in. The room was full of magnificence, creating an atmosphere of great peace as I watched the vision. Pressing in to see more, I somehow knew this was "home," and upon Jesus's beckoning, I watched my young self climb into the Father's lap. Seeing His tight embrace brought on a rush of security in my heart, and I felt as if I were a part of Him. I knew I belonged, I was accepted, I was

His. I knew He would never leave me. Jesus took my hand to leave, and my eyes caught sight of the word ADOPTED in big purple letters on the door. The memory had been completely transformed in a simple instant.

Convinced He had more for me, I kept watching. Another familiar scene streaked across my mind, recapping the memory of being stood-up for a high-school formal—another soul-crushing moment that needed restoration. I watched the scene unfold, seeing myself in a beautiful dress, looking at my tear-stained face in the mirror. The word WORTHLESS written across the middle of the mirror kept me from seeing much of my reflection. In anticipation of something good, I put on the glasses, now with deep purple lenses, that Jesus handed me, changing the scene to one of brilliance and splendor: Jesus and I dancing. I saw profound beauty between the two of us, allowing my soul to come alive from His extravagant love for me, love assuring me of my value and importance in the kingdom. The word in the mirror faded, replaced by the words PRICELESS TREASURE. Unexpected joy poured from my heart as the vision faded. Seeing through the eyes of my Jesus restored my painful memory.

Looking in anticipation, the next scene brought profound sadness: the bedside of my dying sister. Sapping my heart once again, I saw the word LOSS written across the bed. Wondering about any goodness that could come from this, I reluctantly put on the deep purple glasses. Blinking to clear my vision, I saw Jesus and my sister running through a field of wildflowers. Upon her young head, she wore a wreath of lovely blossoms flowing with colorful ribbons that streamed down her back, creating a scene so full of beauty and joy it was breathtaking. With joy on her face, she and Jesus walked away, the word RESTORATION written down the beautiful blue ribbon. I sat quietly, looking at what was now an empty bed. The joy I had just seen inspired me, yet my own desire for her to be here swept over my heart. I noticed an envelope on the bed where she had lain. On the top, it read: "The mysteries of God." When I went to pick it up, it dissolved into flakes of gold, becoming like snow swirling all around me. The gold dust covered my hands as I looked in wonder. Peace covered my soul.

While still in wonder at the meaning of the last vision, Jesus began to lead me, allowing me to see familiar trials and battles of the world I lived in currently. My sensitive heart ached as He led me, yet each time—whether it was a family situation, a struggle in my community, or the pain from living in a lost world—before I could ask, Jesus would hand me the sunglasses that I now understood were giving me access to see through His eyes. Each time I saw restoration, I saw answers, and I saw beauty come from situations that looked hopeless. The long story ended, leaving me a longing to know the mind of Christ.

## The Interpretation

What does it mean to have the mind of Christ? The answer was too large for me to process in one sitting, leading me to interpret the story piece by piece. My cry to God about a financial decision was simply answered by, "Change the way you think." Now I began to understand that God was challenging me to step into the kingdom and see what He sees and to replace the lies of my childhood (being stupid, afraid, abandoned, worthless) with the truth of His heart (being smart, loved, adopted, priceless treasure). That those memories were deeply engrained in my soul meant it would take work to change them—actions requiring repentance and surrender. I began to embrace the truth that the mind of Christ is mine if I choose to access it. The way I see, think, and hear is nothing like His way. I have been given access to a higher kingdom. Would I choose to engage?

Leaning into the mysteries of God would happen through intimacy with Him, which I was drawn to after this vision. Somehow, I loved Him more and longed to see life through His eyes. More than that, I longed for Him and Him alone. I believe He was showing me that the more I trust Him and know His character, the more I am released to gain His wisdom. The mind of Christ is a choice . . . and usually not my first. But if I am going to partner with God in what He is doing, I must first learn to repent of my own thinking and step into His. This would come through learning to receive His love.

Once I believed I was a loved child of God, His daily provision came to my mind. In the case of the financial problem, I needed to step back and remember that I was His child, not an orphan. I needed to reflect on all His provision in my life thus far. This opened my heart to trust and helped me see answers the way He sees them. My broken places began to heal, allowing for kingdom thinking.

As you probably understand by this point in the book, I often allow other people's pain and the distress of the world to overtake me, keeping me from a kingdom mindset. My passion for loving the lost and mentoring the young in discipleship was strong and unencumbered at a young age; however, as life proceeded, I began to only see from my eyes, not His. God challenged me to draw near to Him once again, learning to access the mind of Christ in everything I do. Simply put, to "change the way I think."

I encourage you to process the story again piece by piece, asking God to reveal to you any broken places in your thinking, allowing you to step up into the higher kingdom and to see from the eyes of Jesus. The following activations are actions I began to incorporate more and more in my daily life so I could access the mind of Christ.

## Activations

There are three activations. Read through them and then start where you feel the most led. Take your time. Allow the things that minister to your soul to become a lifestyle, giving you access to the mind of Christ.

### *Activation 1: Transformation*

- Ask the Lord to reveal to you a place in your life where transformation needs to happen and about any wrong thinking that pertains to this place in your life. Write down what comes to mind. If a memory comes up, process through it.

- Ask Holy Spirit for the truth concerning this place in your life, and write out this declaration. For example, "I repent of partnering with the lie that I am not smart. From now on, I will partner with Jesus, stepping into the mind of Christ." Or, "I repent for walking in fear, and I will daily receive the love of Christ, for love casts our fear."

- Using your chosen path, create something that reminds you of truths you have heard from the Holy Spirit. (A few words, a favorite song, a photograph, a letter to yourself.)

- Next time you react to a situation or feel a lie coming up, declare the word of truth you received from the Holy Spirit. Example: "I am deeply loved, therefore I will not fear; I am smart because I have the mind of Christ; I am a priceless treasure belonging to Jesus."

### *Activation 2: The Mysteries of God*

- Write down 1–2 questions from your own life that don't seem to have answers. Ask the Holy Spirit if each question is a problem with an answer, or if it is a mystery of God. The Lord has answers to many of our problems, which can open up for us when we replace our thinking with His. However, some things are mysteries that we simply need to lean into His character about, leading us to trust.

- If you come up with a mystery of God in your life, focus on your heavenly Father and His goodness. Begin to lean into this mystery by acknowledging the goodness of God. Search and write out scriptures pertaining to God's character.

- Lean into the mystery by surrendering it through a simple declaration. For example: "I do not understand the death of my sister, Lord, and as I grieve her loss, I believe that You are a good God, and I entrust this with You."

- Each time you choose to lean into God with a mystery, take time to write down or express what you are hearing. Remember that problems require answers, but the mysteries of God are meant for us to lean into trusting God in order to receive revelation and peace.

### *Activation 3: A Renewed Mind, A Passionate Heart*

- Write down a few things that concern or attract your heart the most, the things you feel deeply—love, fear, peace, passion, or anxiety, things that need an answer or response on what to do about it. Maybe it is in business, education, your family, your finances, your community, the culture, etc. Now ask the Holy Spirit what actions you are to take. Write down a few words or sentences that come to mind.

- Surrender this passion or fear to the Lord, asking for insight in the coming days. For example, "Lord, I am passionate about creating a business that will change people's lives for the better; I want to renew my mind so I can partner with you in the coming days," or "Lord, my child is struggling in school. I pray that he will have the mind of Christ as he goes through his day. Open my ears to a better understanding of how to help him as I entrust him to You."

- Begin a journal to record your progress as you learn to renew your mind daily and listen for His leading.

*"Beloved friends, what should be our proper response to God's marvelous mercies? I encourage you to surrender yourselves to God to be his sacred, living sacrifices. And live in holiness, experiencing all that delights his heart. For this becomes your genuine expression of worship. Stop imitating the ideals and opinions of the culture around you, but be inwardly transformed by the Holy Spirit through a total reformation of how you think. This will empower you to discern God's will as you live a beautiful life, satisfying and perfect in his eyes."*
*Romans 12:1-2*

# CHAPTER FIVE: GLORIOUS PERFECTION

*"But God still loved us with such great love! He is so rich in compassion and mercy. Even when we were dead and doomed in our many sins, he united us into the very life of Christ and saved us by his wonderful grace! He raised us up with Christ the exalted One, and we ascended with him into the glorious perfection and authority of the heavenly realm, for we are now co-seated as one with Christ!"*
*Ephesians 2:4-6*

---

In the complex world we live in, it is easy to compartmentalize our lives, separating secular and spiritual, good and bad, difficult and easy, pain and joy, or love and hate. This often causes us to miss out on the full redemption of our journey that Jesus has for us.

I was in sixth grade as I knelt at the altar in my white lace dress, committing my life to Christ in baptism. I had hoped that heaven would open and an angel would appear or that I would hear the voice of God. When that did not happen, I briefly wondered about the validity of my baptism—a seed of unworthiness planted by the enemy was quietly sown. The supernatural encounter with Jesus that I longed for occurred five years later. While kneeling in the woods alone at camp, I asked Jesus to take over my messy, confused life, and He did. It was just as real as my baptism, yet I knew I had met Jesus. I had stepped into another realm, like stepping into heaven for a moment. The atmosphere around me felt heavy on my skin, yet brought instant peace to my heart. Ten minutes earlier, I had been experiencing loneliness and fear; now the heavenly atmosphere around me and within me brought love and security to my heart. The sweet presence of God stayed with me as I walked back to my cabin, giving me no doubt that the God of heaven had answered my cry. Unfortunately, my performance-based belief system led me to believe it would be up to me to carry out my end of the deal I had just made with God: "I promise to do everything right from now on if You will forgive me and change my life." During the five years after my baptism, self-doubt, lack of identity, and fear had edged into my life and caused anxiety. I deeply desired to excel in life and felt like I was failing.

Without a mentor to guide me correctly, plus the fact that following all the rules was impossible, I slowly separated myself from the God I met in the woods. Not understanding Jesus's unconditional love for me, I believed that every mistake or bad choice I made disqualified me from His sweet presence. I quietly stayed away from God, thinking that He was angry at my inability to get it right: I quit praying; I stayed clear of the college Bible studies; I rarely went to church.

One simple conversation during a counseling session with my pastor turned the table. He simply reminded me of my surrender to Jesus and of His unconditional love for me. As quick as my prayer in the woods, my heart opened to receive fully the love of Jesus. I had gotten it all wrong. There was no "deal" to be made; Jesus loved me and had paid the price for all my sin. I was smitten with this Jesus, and in an instant my life completely transformed. I couldn't wait to meet Jesus in prayer, worship in church, and study His word. My searching for love and joy in the wrong places simply stopped. Passion welled in me to know my Jesus. The teacher gift inside me took this passion to others, bringing life to me as I engaged in His kingdom.

Years and years of life and ministry went by, and I found myself in a peculiar place. I knew the truth, and intimacy with my Savior was my deepest desire, yet my soul was troubled. Anxiety and depression seemed to lurk in the corners, dragging me down like a burdensome covering. I had been created for something great; nonetheless, greatness seemed to be slipping out of sight.

One spring afternoon I was sitting in my front yard, looking at the beautiful new life everywhere. My redbud trees were blooming with exquisite red blossoms, and alluring pink azaleas now covered the usually uninteresting bushes like the most exquisite pink linen. New birth seemed to be everywhere my eyes could behold; however, a plaguing question hovered over my heart. "What is holding me back? Why does my heart remain inaccessible, Lord? You have invited me to surrender all of myself to you, and somehow I cannot find the key to access all of my soul? Why? I know I was created to be great. What is holding me back?"

I closed my eyes and waited for an answer. Another treasure in the form of a story displayed across my mind.

## The Story

A large quantity of brilliant watercolor paintings appeared spread across my driveway. I got up to look and was surprised to see my entire life laid out in the form of vivid images. Some were stunning, bright and radiant; others were dark, dreadful, or dreary. Many spoke of amazing love and laughter; some resonated pain and agony. Each was separate from the other, contrasting the wholesome and the depraved. I saw all of it: my childhood, my college years, my marriage, my children and their growing up years. All of it lay before me on the driveway like a magnificent history book of photographs. I saw the picture of me kneeling in the woods and asking Jesus to come into my heart, as clear as if it were yesterday. Season after season, story after story, lay before me in plain, unobstructed view. As I gazed closer, I noticed that even though the pictures were separate, the dark, gloomy pictures seemed to run off onto the other ones. An optimistic, cheery page was dimmed because of the murky page next to it. As the pages went on, the dark got darker even amongst the beautiful. I looked for a long time, reliving some of the paintings and desperately wishing to tear apart the dark, ugly ones. I speculated, "What would my life be like if I could just get rid of those dreadful pages? Maybe that is what Jesus means when He says new life: erase the dark, and only leave the bright and beautiful."

After a long time, I looked up and saw Him, my Jesus, smiling. All He said was, "You can't separate the story of your life. Every part connects to the next."

"So what do I do, Lord?"

"May I?" He said as if to ask me if He could have all the paintings.

"Yes," I said.

He picked up an unusually large clay jar, as stunning as His eyes, which were the color of the deep sea. Then, tilting the jar, lovely, crystal-clear water, pure as a diamond, poured out, flooding the driveway. The torrent of water mixed the colors into a mesmerizing pool of brilliant paint. Loveliness mixed with the gloomy.

"Now all the paintings will become brown and dreary," I thought, wondering what He was doing.

We watched together as the bright spring sun soaked up all the newly colored water. I felt Jesus's hand in mine as we watched the colors evolve. His lovely smile and penetrating eyes pierced my heart. The most exquisite painting appeared before my eyes. All the pages had fashioned into one vast page, the size of my driveway. It was magnificent. The most meticulous details were intertwined to create a stunning image. I could still see that it was my life, but now it meshed together as one amazingly striking depiction. The dark colors had become the deepest, richest color I have ever seen, with radiant symmetry. Joy, meaning, and purpose exuded from the painting. The depth of the life I saw on the pavement caused me to weep with a questioning heart.

Jesus said, "This is how I make all things new. This is what your life looks like when it is under Me; however, I need every page because the painting will be incomplete without it. Why are you holding on?"

At that moment, for all the world, I could not think of an answer. I opened my eyes and looked at the new life all around me, listening to the birds singing and chirping in joy. I contemplated what I had just experienced.

"Yes, Lord, You may have it all. I may need Your help in finding all those watercolor paintings, for many are hidden away in my soul, but I will give them to You so You can make them all new, magnificent, and divine."

## The Interpretation

The desperate cry of my soul came with an unexpected answer. My inability to walk daily with a renewed mind and heart allowed me to separate my life experiences into compartments, and I simply failed to look at the whole, big, redemptive picture. I loved worshipping, ministry, and my sweet prayer times with the Lord; however, I did not bring the difficult seasons or current struggles to those places. I wanted to deliver myself from darkness, and in that, I failed to allow Jesus to redeem it all, especially my mistakes or my lack of wisdom that created problems in my life. I had all but quit praying about my struggles; all I wanted was "more and more of Jesus."

As I processed through some of the painful seasons of life, I realized how important they were in order for me to notice the true beauty of the other seasons. I had allowed the darkness to rule the light. The seeds of unworthiness were fed by focusing on the seasons of failure, lack, or sin, which birthed my need to perform. Even though I knew Jesus had covered it all with His death, somehow I still believed the lie that my past mistakes had something to do with my value. I knew better, yet I was striving through life.

The pictures on the pavement were so real to me that in an instant I saw my wrong thinking. God wants all of my life. My life is one whole, beautiful picture redeemed by the Lord, not compartments of dark and light. Through repentance, tears, and simple trust, I turned my life over to Jesus one life experience at a time. Slowly, freedom began to ensue as my heart opened to His love. From that point on, the process of restoration began. Where lies came forth, truth emerged, giving me strength and courage to walk forward with great faith and to rid my heart of shame.

Now I see that my past has been rearranged into a fabulous tapestry; it is a dance with God, one in which I am so in step with Him that we are one. What Jesus sees is all that matters, for my inheritance is Him, and I need to grow strong enough to carry all that He has for me. I will have to trust and believe that my "qualifications" are not important and are actually unnecessary. The beauty of a life with God is all about Him. When the enemy brings up my past or a current struggle, I simply tell him about the poetry of my redeemed life, one that has been recreated by the Master himself.

The following activations were a few of the steps I walked through to process this vision.

## Activations

There are three activations. Read through them and then start where you feel the most led. Take your time. Allow the things that minister to your soul to become a lifestyle, giving you access to the mind of Christ.

### Activation 1: Seasons of Your Life

- Rewrite Ephesians 2:4–6 in your own words, inserting your own name.

- What season are you experiencing right now in your life? For example: the desert or wilderness, darkness or light, one of vision, passion, goodness, glory, and abundance, etc.

- When you have taken note of the season and the condition of your heart, write down one line that paints a picture of this current season, using at least four descriptive words. Then invite God to be in the middle of it, and thank Him, believing the promise of redemption for every part of your life.

- Take time to review the "watercolor pictures" of your life. Ask the Holy Spirit to bring to your memory as many parts of your life as you can think of. Allow your mind to wander through the paintings of each season or specific events, good and bad.

- Write down the pictures that seem highlighted to you, creating a life map.

- Write one or two words that describe your feelings in those seasons. Be honest. If you find anger, write it down. If there is shame, write it down. If there is joy, write it down.

- Focus on all the good things you see on your life map: promises fulfilled, joy, answers to prayers. Write out a testimony of the goodness of God, and commit to share it with others. Ask God to reveal to you in the coming days who might need to hear this evidence of the power of God in your life.

## *Activation 2: Darkness*

- Read Ephesian 2:1-13, and write down or discuss whether you know this passage is true, or whether you believe it is true in your life.

- Go back through your life map, looking for the dark emotions and words that are separated or unredeemed. Surrender these dark places by writing out a statement of faith. For example, "Lord, I give you this place in my life. I repent for _____. I receive your redemption and invite you to bring new life to it." Or, "Lord, forgive me for separating and compartmentalizing my life. I ask you to bring it together as one new life, giving me greater power to walk in the way You are calling."

- This may take a moment; it may take days. Walk through each one, surrendering any darkness and pain to Him. (If you have completed the "Tears" section, you may have already done this part. Go back and review anything in that session that might be helpful.)

- As you surrender any shame, sadness, and pain in your life, open your hands as a release to God. Have faith to leave it with Him, and next time the enemy brings it up, remind him that it is gone—it has been transformed.

## *Activation 3: Recreation*

- Close your eyes and ask God to show you your life as He sees it. You may see words, colors, or shapes. It may come to you in a parable or just a knowing.

- Using your creative path, create your life as it looks after being redeemed. This might look like one word or a list of words, it might be a beautiful photograph of a place you love or long to visit, a song you know or one you write, a poem or even a love letter from God, a favorite scripture or a new one recently revealed to you, something simple yet full of meaning for you.

- Look at the created picture of your life. Write a prayer of thanks for the beauty of your renewed life, and refuse to identify yourself with anything other than this. Your identity is never in your sin or temptation; your identity is in Jesus. For example, I found a picture of my favorite lake to represent my renewed life, and I created this statement to go with it:

"Jesus has recreated my life to be full of beauty, laughter, and joy, as I am His. I carry the presence of God with me, drawing others to Him. Like the beautiful green waters that flow through the lake, I am always changing, growing more and more like Jesus. The challenges and struggles of my life, like the rugged cliffs on the lake, are the very things that bring more beauty, laughter, and joy. I am the poetry of God."

- Allow yourself to be bold even if it doesn't seem true to you now. Put this in an accessible place so that every time you are tempted to identify yourself as a failure or according to your past sins, you can say no and read this statement out loud.

- Read Ephesians 2:10 in two different translations. Write down what it means to you for your life to become "His poetry" that will fulfill the destiny He has chosen for you, and give thanks to God for the recreation of your life.

*"His lovely smile and penetrating eyes pierced my heart. The most exquisite painting appeared before my eyes. . . . The dark colors had become the deepest, richest color I have ever seen, with radiant symmetry. Joy, meaning, and purpose exuded from the painting."*

## CHAPTER SIX: WAIT

*"Trust in the Lord, and do good; Dwell in the land, and feed on His faithfulness.*
*Delight yourself also in the Lord, And He shall give you the desires of your heart.*
*Commit your way to the Lord, Trust also in Him, And He shall bring it to pass.*
*He shall bring forth your righteousness as the light, And your justice as the noonday.*
*Rest in the Lord, and wait patiently for Him; Do not fret because of him who prospers in his way,*
*Because of the man who brings wicked schemes to pass. Cease from anger,*
*and forsake wrath; Do not fret—it only causes harm."*
*Psalm 37:3-8 NKJV*

---

In the culture of speed and instant gratification the actions of resting and waiting patiently are rare. For many, hard work and perseverance are easier to accomplish than resting and waiting. Part of my journey included learning to wait and finding great joy while resting in the Lord.

Psalm 37 is one of my favorite passages of Scripture. I love to camp out there over and over. "Take delight in the Lord, and He will give you the desires of your heart. . . . Be still before the Lord and wait patiently for him."

The meaning of this passage became important in my life several years ago when my husband and I, along with our three young boys, lived in Katy, Texas, a large suburb outside of Houston. As the city grew, bringing more and more traffic, our daily commute became long and laborious. I began to ask the Lord about the possibility of moving closer to town—silence was all I encountered. Over time, my prayers turned into begging and then to a declaration: "Lord, since I don't hear You on this subject, I believe it is okay to move." The closest I have ever gotten to the audible voice of God came next. I heard, "Psalm 37," in the depths of my heart.

Opening my Bible to Psalm 37, the word *wait* jumped off the page. I read the passage over and over, hoping for a different result, but the word that day was *wait*. I had no explanation or reason, just wait. So, because waiting longer than two days seemed like a long time, I waited six weeks. The day I scheduled a realtor to come look at my house to sell, I got a call. My sister, who lived five minutes away, had been life-flighted to the hospital; she had had a brain aneurysm. Over the next year her husband would spend his days at the hospital, rehab, and work, leaving Thomas, their youngest son and a freshman in high school, in need of guidance. It is amazing how quickly life can change our thinking. For the next three years we would try to stand in for the missing place of my sister in her family as best as we could. The idea of moving ceased to exist. It never even occurred to me as an option or even a desire.

I would not venture back to Psalm 37 until three years later when Thomas was graduating from high school and heading to college. I sat down with my Bible and happened on Psalm 37—"wait." Tears began to flow freely as I saw God's beautiful provision. We needed to wait so we could be close by. I would not have given away those three years for anything. My sister and I had promised one another to care for each other's children if something happened to us. Something had happened. Tears of thanksgiving flowed, and three years after the first prayer, I finally felt the release to move.

My oldest son, Luke, was heading into the eighth grade, so we decided to wait a year until he was in high school to move, allowing plenty of time for our house to sell. This time, however, God was saying, "Go." At the end of August, after we got Thomas to college and just before Luke's eighth grade year, our realtor called to tell us he had a buyer for our house—as is, all cash. The house was not even on the market yet. Two weeks before school started we moved in with my parents, and three months later we were in the house and neighborhood we dreamed of. It became a place of ministry where hundreds of children and teens played, partied, and worshipped, a place of joy, love, and laughter for our family. Yes, indeed, He brought it to pass all in His perfect timing.

Many years later, I found myself in a different place. After over fifteen years on staff at a church, I felt the Lord prompting me to quit, to move on. With grown children and many dreams still on the horizon, as well as a desire to love my aging parents well, I quit my job. I had grown up at this church: I got married there, raised my children there, volunteered in every area possible, worked on staff. Stepping away felt painful, yet needed. My husband had a great job in oil and gas, so we would be fine without my job. Soon after I quit, with oil prices plummeting, all in one day his company closed down. This was not what we had dreamed of, nor planned for. Had I misunderstood about quitting my job? Had I been too quick to quit?

I was not afraid, for God has always been my rock, my provider all my life. Bumps in the road and hardships come along, always challenging us to strengthen our faith and prepare for the blessings ahead. However, after a year of no work, my dreams seemed to be slipping out of view. God was silent, so I opened to Psalm 37 once more: "Delight yourself also in the Lord, and He shall give you the desires of your heart." I wondered if I had missed the point. I wasn't in my thirties anymore. The clock seemed to be ticking faster, and my dreams growing dimmer. The best way I knew to delight in Jesus was to worship, so I put on worship music and lay down on the ground, and He gave me treasure in the form of a vision.

## The Story

I saw a man coming towards me—Jesus. I recognized Him because of His eyes: the color of the ocean full of the world. He took my hand, and together we began to run unencumbered through a field. The field was beautiful, bursting with fresh smells and vivid colors. To my delight, His face was full of boundless joy. My heart felt full, wondering where we might be going.

At the end of the field we came to the base of a never-ending, steep mountain. He spoke for the first time, "Follow Me." The climb up this ominous mountain, with steep, rocky, and treacherous terrain, was challenging, but seemed easy as long as my focus was on Jesus. Looking down was not an option as we climbed for what seemed like hours or even days. Not wanting to deviate off the path, my eyes stayed glued to His feet, and I copied His every move.

We reached the top together, finding a soundless sky and a spectacular, out-of-this-world view. Peace fell upon my soul as I took it all in. Even when He summoned me to the edge, there was no fear. As I took His hand, we looked out over the edge of the mountain, and to my surprise, down in the valley miles and miles away, I could see clear as day my desires, my dreams, and my destiny all laid out before my eyes, a complex view that somehow incorporated every dream I have ever desired and much more. It began small with my family, children, grandchildren, and great-grandchildren, expanding to more family, friends, my church, city, and nation, all that I could think or imagine. The past, the future was all there. Where there was pain, I felt joy; where there was chaos, I felt peace. Most of all, the love of Jesus flooded my soul as I gazed upon this scene.

I laughed as He smiled and asked me, "Would you like to go there?"

"Yes, yes, You know I would, Lord. Those are my dreams."

He took my hand, and we started down the mountain together. Immediately, I became aware of the abruptness of the steep hill. Mesmerized by what lay at the bottom, I did not notice the vertical drop going on forever in front of me, the memory of the long, difficult climb up completely forgotten. Holding His hand, we carefully made our way over the rocks and through the crevices. Occasionally letting go and looking away, I would focus on the difficulty of the journey. At those moments, Jesus appeared to vanish, ushering in fear and fatigue like a fire. Looking down, I could no longer see where I was going, causing me to close my eyes and cry out in sheer panic. Opening my eyes, I saw Jesus, sitting away in a lovely green pasture surrounded by a gated fence. I was not sure where the pasture had come from, but I was happy to be on level ground and once again in the presence of my Jesus. My fear and panic fled; His smile causing love to fill my soul. Once I got close, I noticed a lock on the gate. There would be no more forward progress without a key. In dismay I asked, "Is this what has stopped me from the desires of my heart?" As He smiled I felt Him say yes.

Before I could be disheartened, the Lord begin to dance with me. We danced and ran and played on the green grass, and as I did, my heart raced with joy, the locked gate and menacing cliff all but disregarded. Wind in my hair under the bright sun brought a sweet childlike freedom to my heart and soul. Falling to the ground in hilarious laughter, bliss overcame me. His love for me was beyond anything I had ever known, and as I delighted in Him, my love for Him grew stronger and stronger. After what seemed like hours, days, or weeks, I dropped to the ground to rest, and as I did a key fell out of my pocket. The word AUTHORITY was written on it. He smiled. I asked Him, "Is this the key to the gate?" He nodded yes. At that moment, I realized by the look in His eyes that it had been in my pocket all along, and I just did not know it. I could not know it until, in our delight together, I could begin to see how much the God of heaven really loved me. I actually was precious to Him. I had gained the authority to open the gate through my delight in Him.

We opened the gate and went through, only to find more challenges. The giant rocks became my focus, causing me to lose sight of Jesus once again. Panic, fear, and a call for help ensued. A beautiful landing, love, laughter, and fun with Jesus followed—and then another key. One time on the landing I ministered to Him. He seemed tired, and I cared for Him. At other landings, we laughed and played and sometimes cried together. Crying with Him was an altogether different experience, because when I cried with Him, it seemed we were crying for the nations of the world. I completely forgot about myself, my own dreams and ideas, and stepped into the pain of the world that my sweet Savior carried. Another time He began to show me His dreams for the world. I was overcome with the immensity of His dreams, the fulfillment of something so amazing and beautiful. I was speechless that He would allow me to vision with Him. Each time, after what seemed like days or weeks of delighting in Him, weeping with Him, dreaming with Him, I would fall to the ground and a key would fall out of my pocket, the keys I didn't know I had to open the gate. AUTHORITY was written on every key.

At the opening of each new gate I grew stronger and my heart grew very attached to His. I found myself looking at the steep mountain descent less and less. Occasionally, I would look down and fear would flood in, but I was quicker to find Him each time. While the vision of dreams in the valley was hard to see much of the trip down, He would always help me focus on what I was running toward each time we opened a new gate. That would give me the strength to go down yet another steep and stony mountainside.

Unlocking a gate one more time, I found myself standing in awe. My past, present, and future all swirled around me in perfect harmony. As I looked up, I saw only blessing, and as I looked forward, I saw there was more to come. As sure and strong as the noonday sun, I stood in the middle of blessing overflowing. I realized that the vision was all in the journey. I knelt to the ground and kissed the feet of my Savior, for I knew it was all about Him.

At the top He said, "Rest in the Lord and wait patiently for Him and He will bring it to pass."

Yes, indeed, He had.

## The Interpretation

While waiting on anything has never been my strong suit, the idea of delighting in the Lord has always captivated me. But what did it really mean to delight in the Lord? Do I really believe He cares about the desires of my heart? What are the desires of my heart, and why am I called to wait? At first the story seemed obvious to me. I believed that keeping my eyes on Jesus during the difficult times would give me the strength and authority I needed to move toward my destiny and dreams. I looked back on my experience in Katy, Texas, and saw joy and peace in my times with the Lord. Was that delight? I saw the heartache, comfort, wonder, and blessing all mixed together in those years. Was that delight? I saw the waiting—from this point of view it was effortless and easy. I saw the joy and happiness that came with the honor of participating with my sister's family. Was that delight? Delighting in the Lord brought freedom: freedom to trust, freedom to dream, freedom to love and minister to others. That delight was building a deep passion to see what God was doing in the middle of it all. Even through the struggle that I described in the "Tears" chapter, I found delight in my Jesus.

The more I processed the vision, I realized there was much more to it than just that interpretation. I took a closer look at what was really happening on those grassy landings where Jesus and I played and danced together. The idea of freely dancing, running, or playing with Jesus, as beautiful as it sounds, was not a reality in my life. I wondered if Jesus showed up in my room right now, would I be able to dance or play with Him? My heart said no, causing me to dig for what was holding me back. Fear, self-doubt, performance, striving would all present themselves and keep me from the freedom of truly delighting in my Savior. Once again, the question stirred: Why are they there? I closed my eyes and looked at the vision again, asking the Lord to highlight something to me. He showed me my face: it looked like a child's, with joy and full-on laughter. When was the last time I laughed like that, really laughed?

A child playing on a cliff with a trusted, beloved father would not have fear. Complete trust would allow the child to laugh, play, and see the cliff as adventure. Did I do that? Could I do that? I closed my eyes again and asked God to show me the same scene through my adult eyes. I saw the giant mountain, the steep cliff, the extremely long way left in front of us, and all those gates, seemingly hundreds of them. This was the struggle. In the vision, Jesus never even seemed concerned about any of those things, just about me. Clearly most of my life I had not given myself permission to delight in my Savior, for I had been trying to be Him.

Delighting in Jesus was not something I could strive to do for Him; it was what He longed to do with me. He is my Father and protector, my comforter and guide, my shield and refuge, my healer waiting for me to delight in Him, waiting for me to receive all that He has for me. Could it be that much of my life I have believed I was alone, trying to provide for myself? Had I been so happy to receive salvation, yet failed to receive all of Jesus? I imagined what it would be like to just enjoy my heavenly Father even in the midst of struggle. This seemed difficult, but I knew Jesus was telling me it is not: "Just come and allow me to be your Father, a good, good Father." To delight was to trust, to turn it over to Him, all of it, to allow Him to love me. As I pondered this I realized I had not given myself permission to be joyful with Him for a very, very long time. Stress had become my partner and even my protection, causing me to believe I did not have time to dance with my Savior, for clearly there was work to be done. Once again, my mind and spirit knew better, but my soul had taken control. My dreams were not disappearing. I simply was stuck on the cliff because of my need to control and self-protect.

The Lord is calling me to delight in Him, to find joy in the smallest gifts given daily as I let go of fear. He is the perfect Father and all my dreams are attached to Him. Courage will follow, identity will become clear, and it is then I will find the authority that He has given me to move forward.

No one gets to slide down the mountain effortlessly. Cliffs appear without warning, giving very little time to respond, but God has provided a way. He is not asking me to buck up with my own self-discipline. He is showing me how to grow up by trusting in Him every step of the way. As I wait on Him, like a daughter would love on a Father, He is present with me, strengthening me for the next part of the journey. I watch my son Luke with his baby daughter: her eyes light up and she laughs out loud when he enters the room. Pure, innocent love for her daddy. This is what God desires from me, His daughter. My dreams are not the end result; they are part of the process. As I keep delighting in Him, I fall deeper in love with my God, the One who invites me to partner with His dreams, His immeasurable, impossible, beautiful, magnificent dreams.

After repenting with tears of thanksgiving, I stepped back up to the gate currently in my life with my eyes focused directly on Him, Jesus. I already have the key.

"The joy of the Lord is my strength and shield." (Psalm 28:7 NLT)

By doing the activations below, I have continued in my process of renewing my heart and mind, this time allowing myself to receive what He has for me each day, leading me to dream for the impossible.

## Activations

There are three activations. Read through them and then start where you feel the most led. Take your time. Allow the things that minister to your soul to become a lifestyle, giving you access to the mind of Christ.

## Activation 1: Dreams

"Never doubt God's mighty power to work in you and accomplish all this. He will achieve infinitely more than your greatest request, your most unbelievable dream, and exceed your wildest imagination! He will outdo them all, for His miraculous power constantly energizes you." (Ephesians 3:20)

- Create a list of 50-100 dreams from your heart. They can be for yourself, your family, your church, your community, your nation, the world. Do not think about the possibility or impossibility of them, just write down what is on your heart. If you are stuck, take a walk or spend time praising the Lord, thanking Him for what He has done in your life and during your lifetime in the world. Keep working on the list throughout the next week until you have 100. If you have more, go for it!

- Highlight the most imminent dreams that seem crucially important to you right now. The ones your heart desires most. Then pick one. Close your eyes and visualize what it looks like fulfilled.

- Ask yourself, "What is in the way of my dream?" Write out everything that blocks the path, anything causing fear, pain, or hopelessness toward that dream. Check your heart for anger or bitterness. Be honest and write it down if it is there.

- Go back and look at your list of promises fulfilled and the faithfulness of God in your life. Write them as a testimony next to every block you found today. Allow the Lord to restore hope to you as you focus on Him.

- Ask the Lord to show you one of His dreams for your life or for the world. This may come to you in a moment or over time. Pay attention to what is pulling on your heart as you go through your day.

- Look back at your dreams. Is there a place where your dreams come together with this dream of His? Write out a prayer of courage and faith that positions you to step in and partner with God in His dream.

## Activation 2: Up the Mountain

"Keep Trusting in the Lord and do what is right in His eyes. Fix your heart on the promises of God and you will be secure, Feasting on His faithfulness."

- Imagine your life as a mountain-climbing adventure. Look back at your seasons of life map and graph your life on paper. Ask the Lord to show you key places where your heart was fixed on His promises, therefore keeping you secure along the path.

- Write out where Jesus was at each pivotal point during your climb.

- Using your creative path or writing in your journal, create something that describes His faithfulness over your life so far.

## Activation 3: Delight and Rest

- Read the following scriptures. After each one close your eyes and put yourself into the scripture. Invite Jesus to come alongside you. After each one, write down what He is saying to you about delighting in Him.

  "Seize life! Eat bread with gusto,
  Drink wine with a robust heart.
  Oh yes—God takes pleasure in your pleasure!
  Dress festively every morning.
  Don't skimp on colors and scarves.
  Relish life with the spouse you love
  Each and every day of your precarious life.
  Each day is God's gift."
  (Ecclesiastes 9:7–8 MSG)

  "Now may God, the inspiration and fountain of hope, fill you to overflowing with uncontainable joy and perfect peace as you trust in him. And may the power of the Holy Spirit continually surround your life with his super-abundance until you radiate with hope!" (Romans 15:13)

"For the kingdom of God is not a matter of rules about food and drink, but is in the realm of the Holy Spirit, filled with righteousness, peace, and joy. Serving the Anointed One by walking in these kingdom realities pleases God and earns the respect of others." (Romans 14:17-18)

"As the Father loved Me, I also have loved you; abide in My love. If you keep My commandments, you will abide in My love, just as I have kept My Father's commandments and abide in His love. These things I have spoken to you that My joy may remain in you, and that your joy may be full." (John 15:9-11 NKJV)

"Then those 'sheep' are going to say, 'Master, what are you talking about? When did we ever see you hungry and feed you, thirsty and give you a drink? And when did we ever see you sick or in prison and come to you?' Then the King will say, 'I'm telling the solemn truth: Whenever you did one of these things to someone overlooked or ignored, that was me—you did it to me.'" (Matthew 25:40 MSG)

- Ask yourself these questions:
    Do you have a childlike love for and trust in your heavenly Father?
    Have you been trying to carry all the weight and do it yourself?
    Have you been trying to be the Savior?
    What steps must you take to become like a child with Him?

- Spend time to rest and delight with your Lord. Do not look at the cliff and what lies ahead; just focus your heart, mind, and soul on Jesus in the way He is calling you. Sit quietly and listen, or read Scripture, possibly starting in the Psalms until you find peace, or listen to worship music. Do anything that makes you stop, be still, and listen. This might be doing something you love or something that makes you laugh and inviting His presence as you do.

- Look back at your list for a dream or promise that you are waiting for right now, and then read Psalm 37 again in your favorite translation. Use your chosen creative path to form a picture of what it means to you to delight in the Lord, to "rest in the Lord, and wait patiently for Him" to fulfill that dream in your life.

*"Unlocking a gate one more time, I found myself standing in awe. My past, present, and future all swirled around me in perfect harmony. As I looked up, I saw only blessing, and as I looked forward, I saw there was more to come. As sure and strong as the noonday sun, I stood in the middle of blessing overflowing. I realized that the vision was all in the journey. I knelt to the ground and kissed the feet of my Savior, for I knew it was all about Him."*

## CHAPTER SEVEN: THE RICHES IN GLORY

*"And I pray that he would unveil within you the unlimited riches of his glory and favor until supernatural strength floods your innermost being with his divine might and explosive power. Then, by constantly using your faith, the life of Christ will be released deep inside you, and the resting place of his love will become the very source and root of your life. Then you will be empowered to discover what every holy one experiences— the great magnitude of the astonishing love of Christ in all its dimensions. How deeply intimate and far-reaching is his love! How enduring and inclusive it is! Endless love beyond measurement that transcends our understanding—this extravagant love pours into you until you are filled to overflowing with the fullness of God! Never doubt God's mighty power to work in you and accomplish all this. He will achieve infinitely more than your greatest request, your most unbelievable dream, and exceed your wildest imagination! He will outdo them all, for his miraculous power constantly energizes you! Now we offer up to God all the glorious praise that rises from every church in every generation through Jesus Christ—and all that will yet be manifest through time and eternity. Amen!"*

*Ephesians 3:16-21*

---

We live in a world where exceptional performance is required for success. Young children are thrown into competition as school, sports, and even siblings put pressures on young souls to achieve. Awards are given at the end of the school year, bringing acclamation to one or two, leaving many to keep striving for success or wondering about their own value. Top scores are required for college. The best teams, the best athletes, and the top businesses are applauded and labeled successful. Even churches begin to focus on how many seats are filled instead of souls saved and lives changed. Social media challenges us to compete with one another to look the best, travel the most, and find perfection in our daily lives. Our world tells us there is not enough for everyone. It requires proof for worthiness and significance, which in reality is a never-ending and impossible task. Yet, living in this world, we can easily fall into the mode of striving in our effort to be known and loved by God. No matter what season of life, the need to fight for our place begins to seep its way into our identity if we are not daily resting in the love of our heavenly Father.

As I stepped into a different season where most of my life's vocation had changed, I found out quickly that much of my identity was attached to my life's assignments—something I would have denied months earlier. I felt disoriented, as if my purpose had been suddenly stripped away even though I knew better.

My children had grown into beautiful young adults, no longer needing my daily mothering skills. Most of my adult life had been purposed to raising my children, and while I felt great joy at the amazing adults they had become, my own identity was apparently in crisis. At the leading of the Lord and after a lifetime of ministry, I was no longer working on staff at church, and my husband was going through his own season of change with no job. We were both floundering, asking the Lord what we were supposed to be doing.

It became clear that change was needed before I could move on, for no doors were opening. Listening for God to show me what He wanted me to do, I purposed myself to worship, pray, and pour over the Word.

Silence. God was calling me to being, not doing.

The only thing I heard was "rest." Rest does not come easy for me. Resting required me to be quiet and listen, to stop and really hear what the Lord was saying. The Lord was calling me to Himself. While raising three boys, there were times when it seemed like the train of our lives was moving so fast that we just might roll right off the track; now God seemingly had pulled the tracks out from under us and stopped the entire train. He was summoning us into a higher season, but there were adjustments to be made before we would be prepared for what God had for us.

In the midst of a busy life of cultivating a marriage relationship, intentional parenting to my children, working in ministry, and loving others, I had simply not been tending to my own soul, my own heart, and my own mind. This oversight allowed erosion in all areas of my life that needed the tender love of the Father, the healing of my sweet Jesus, and the power and insight of the Holy Spirit. Somehow, I had forgotten that I am part of a superior kingdom—that is my calling. I am to live from that point of view, from the wealth of another kingdom. I would need to spend some significant time with Jesus in order to go deeper.

One morning while reading the powerful words of Ephesians 3, I felt the Holy Spirit ask me if I really believed them. Was I walking with supernatural strength and explosive power? Contemplating over my life, I saw many powerful works of God in my life and ministry. Our family and ministry were full of testimonies of the wondrous works of a mighty and loving God, but at the moment I had fallen in the dark. I simply prayed, "Lord, what are the riches of Your glory?" Once again, the Lord answered with another treasure for my soul.

## The Story

I met Him at the door. The door was large and white, just a simple door. On the door was a sign with a single word: GLORY.

"Lord," I asked, "what is Your glory?"

He quietly answered, "Limitless riches."

As He opened the door, I saw black darkness. I grabbed His hand for protection in my fear. As I looked at Him, His face was not sad, nor worried; it was full of great joy. Could it be that He could see something I could not? Without words, He led me inside, inviting me to trust Him to see what He was seeing.

The first step I saw beauty more grandiose than words could describe. Effervescent colors on a path led us to a river. The sandy-bottomed river was exquisite, gorgeous beyond what I had ever seen or experienced, the glass-like water running quietly over stones made of beautiful gems: blue sapphires, sparkling diamonds, and every color of stone, many I have never seen before. I stepped into the river and knelt down and ran my hands through the golden sand.

"The wealth of the kingdom," He said.

The river went on as far as my eyes could see. I looked at His face as if to say, "May I?"

"Of course," He said as He laughed with intense joy. "What is mine is yours."

I began to fill my pockets with precious stones, and as I put them in, I found there was no limit to my pockets. As I filled my pockets, I began to feel a sense of importance and great value. No matter how much I put in, I still had room for more! He summoned me to continue on.

We ran through the river and came to a colorful waterfall, and there we began to dance in the water like children. As I danced and laughed, I felt my strength gaining and all the pain, sadness, and fear I had experienced in my life thus far washed off into the golden sand. The heaviness and the weight of life I had been carrying simply washed away. I wondered, "Could it be this easy?"

On His face, I saw the answer. "No, it is not easy." I saw Him looking at something at the top of the hill. I followed His gaze and saw a vision: Jesus hanging on a cross. All the pain that had just washed off of me was now on Him. He looked at me and said, "Do you see how much I love you?"

Before I could respond, He grabbed my hand and took me deeper into the waterfall. We stepped into a cave where everything around us sparkled—the floor, the walls, all of it dazzling. I saw smaller rivers, each a different color, running off the main river. These smaller tributaries bent around and somehow ran higher, creating the waterfall of colors. At the base of each river were words made out of gemstones. There were more than I could read, but some of those I saw read: JOY, LAUGHTER, HEALING, LIFE, and in dark red, LOVE. Deeper we continued down the river.

Soon we came upon a most glorious place, an aquamarine pool full of fascinating bottles, millions and millions of bottles half-buried in the golden sand. I could tell this was a sacred place, and I fell to my knees. I looked into His eyes and saw tears, yet He nodded at my desire to pick up a bottle. On the bottle I selected was my name, and in large print it read: TEARS. When I looked at Him in wonder, He explained, "Your tears are part of my glorious riches. I paid the price for everyone. They are my treasure." I was in awe that my Savior had saved every tear I had ever shed. I realized that every bottle had a name, and there, in this sacred place, the tears of His children were stored. I set the bottle down, and we ran forward hand-in-hand.

On our journey I saw trees, large and majestic and vibrant with color. On the trees were many words like: WISDOM, PROPHECY, DISCERNMENT, MYSTERIES OF GOD. As I touched each tree, I began to be more alive than I had ever been in my lifetime. I could see, touch, hear, and know truth. It was as if all at once I knew the story; in that moment, I could feel pain, not my own, but the pain of the world. However, the pain was being held by someone else, and I felt intense satisfaction knowing what I had never known before.

We continued through the river into a place of penetrating peace. As far as the eye could see were trees full of white doves growing out of lush green grass. Jesus was revealing His nature to me as we walked together, and at each new revelation I began to know myself in that same way.

Although the pain of the world I had gained from the colorful trees was still present, I was completely at peace. We came to a mountain and began to climb. I found my strength gaining as we reached the summit. There are not words to describe what I saw, but it was so spectacular that I held on to Him for fear I might die at the sight—vibrant colors shining through what looked like crystal walls. It was from here that the river and all its beauty and riches flowed. Looking out at the flowing river, I could see all the nations of the world. It was washing over them, bringing the possibility of glory and fullness to each one. As I looked closer, I could see that many places and people in the nations were not accessing the river and all its wealth, yet it was running right in front of them. How could they not see it?

Before I could ask, I turned, and we were at the large white door again, this time on the inside. On this side of the door were two signs. One read GRACE and the other FAVOR. He summoned to me to turn the knob. When I reluctantly touched it, FAVOR was written on my arm. I understood: Because of His grace, I would have favor to the unlimited riches of His glory that I had just seen. I have access to it, "But how, Lord? How do I access all this on the other side of this door? I have been there, and it's not like this."

He smiled. "It will come by faith. You have access as you use your faith. As you trust Me, My love will become the very source and root of your life."

As I stepped out on the other side of the door, I fell to the ground because of the weight of the unlimited supply of wealth, knowledge, life, and love with which I had filled my pockets. I simply could not stand up with the weight of His glory.

"I will carry it," He said. "You may access it with your faith, and if you do, you will begin to carry the great magnitude of my love in your soul. This endless love will continue to pour into you until you are overflowing with the fullness of God.

I nodded, yet did not understand. Before the door closed, He asked me to look back to the rivers, the forest, and the mountain one more time, and I saw in a flash more than my mind could conceive. I saw entire nations covered with the river of God. I saw myself gaining strength and joy through His miraculous power. I saw myself full of His authority, ready to face any battle. But what I saw next changed me forever.

As I looked closer, I realized that what I was seeing was within Him. This was all part of Him. The unlimited riches of glory were God Himself: He is my inheritance. I stood and gazed at the beauty and wonder, overwhelmed by the very thought of such intimacy with God.

We turned, and as the door closed, I knew I had received favor to obtain all that He had paid the price for, all that I had seen and more. It would be up to me about how much I wanted to participate.

As I walked away, the angels of heaven were singing the most glorious praise to the King of Kings. In my pocket one small diamond was left. As I turned it over in my hand, a beautiful white dove landed on my shoulder.

## The Interpretation

This story jolted me. I realized I had been floundering in life. Somewhere along the path of parenting, teaching, ministering, of being a wife to my husband and a daughter to my parents, I had lost sight of who I was and gotten caught up in performance and outcomes, striving to live instead of living out of my identity. While my assignments in life may fade away or change, I will always and forever be a daughter of the King of Kings, a child of the living God.

Looking at my new baby granddaughter, June, reminds me how to be a daughter. When her daddy and mommy walk in the room, her little face lights up, for unconditional love and perfect provision are hers. She knows her parents and that all they have belongs to her now and forever, yet she won't be driving the car or getting an allowance today. She will grow stronger as her daddy and mommy pour into her life daily, causing her to feel known and loved. As parents, they will intentionally make themselves famous to her with a desire for her to grow up knowing that she is a Withers, living by a certain set of core values and, most importantly, growing to know her God.

For me, as a daughter of the living God, I have access to all of Him. There is no greater identity than belonging to Him, knowing Him, and being known by Him. Just like my sweet baby June will never need to perform for her daddy's love, neither do I. I am His, therefore not only do I receive His abundant and extravagant love, I inherit His love for this world. I have access to the power and glory I need to partner with Him in loving the world. The unlimited supply of an extravagant kingdom is mine. My access to it comes with my surrender to lean into my Father's love even when I am disappointed, tired, or sad. Trusting Him in the dark seasons will grow my faith and capacity to carry His riches.

In answering my question about God's riches, this vision was a reminder of who I am, and although I knew this truth through years of sweet intimacy with Him, striving had set in, causing me to lose sight of the path.

After working through this vision, I spent time repenting for competing or toiling for His love and acceptance. That seems absolutely ridiculous to me now. How could I lose sight of the wealth of the kingdom I am part of? God did not tell me what to do next; He simply reminded me that I am His precious daughter and that all He has is mine. Freedom to dream again with that beautiful river in mind is slowly pressing in. As I go forward to the next season, I must be prepared for the battle, knowing I am on the winning team. Forgetting who I am and wandering away from my God is not an option.

I challenge you to open your heart to the limitless riches of God. Do you know who you are? Are you living like a son or daughter of the King of Kings? Take some time to go through these activations, focusing on your capacity for God's love for you. Then take the challenge of seeing where He is calling you today, knowing He will provide everything you need no matter how impossible the task.

## Activations

There are four activations. Read through them and then start where you feel the most led. Take your time. Allow the things that minister to your soul to become a lifestyle, giving you access to the mind of Christ.

### *Activation 1: The Door*

- Take time to ask some honest questions. Do not overthink them; just write what comes to mind, first allowing your heart to lead.

    Who am I?

    What are my successes? My failures?

    What are some of my greatest temptations?

    Which of these things—my success, my failure, my temptation—define me in any way?

    Where am I stuck? Where do I feel free?

    What dream is on my heart?

    If Jesus invited me to step into heaven and experience His glorious riches, would anything hold me back? If so, what is it?

- Spend some time in prayer asking the Lord to show you what you believe about your identity. Focus on your answers, allowing Jesus to show you where He wants you to be transformed. Write these things down.

## *Activation 2: His Riches*

- Favor is written on your heart because of His love for you. Because of His grace, you have favor to the unlimited riches of His glory. You access them by faith. As you activate your faith and trust in Him, His love will become the very source and root of your life.

- Read Ephesians 3:16-21 in your favorite translation.

- Read over the activation and then take a walk outside or simply find a quiet space. Before you begin, close your eyes and ask the Holy Spirit to pour over you His unlimited riches until supernatural strength floods your innermost being. Focus on God as you walk or sit quietly.

- Take note of what you see with your natural eyes and what you hear with your natural ears, and then ask God to speak to your spirit. Don't strive to hear or see or feel anything; just walk and trust, allowing God to refresh your soul. Imagine His divine might and explosive power overtaking your life. Describe what this might look like to you. Once again, don't get stuck here; just keep walking and focusing on Him.

- Stop along the way. Ask God for torrents of His glory to flow over you. Again, do not worry or strive to feel, see, or hear anything; only trust that He is working in you.

- When you are done with your walk, spend a moment writing about your walk. If one word comes to mind, write it down and thank God for it. This is a gift just for you.

- After your walk or quiet time with Jesus, answer these questions:
    What are your spiritual and emotional pockets full of? What riches are you carrying?
    Do you need to let go of some things before you can access by faith these amazing riches?
    Take time now to empty your pockets. Repent where you need to.
    Go back and answer the questions from the first activation. Have any of them changed?
    How might your life change from living out of your true identity instead of living to create it?

- Do this exercise as often as you can throughout your week.

## Activation 3: The Cross

- Find a quiet place. Read Isaiah 53:1–10.

- Ask the Lord to show you what He died for in your life. Wait quietly and listen.

- Turn what He shows you into a love letter to you from Him, and use your preferred path to write the letter.

## Activation 4: Extravagant Love

- Focus on the Words:
  *Joy   Laughter   Healing   Life   Love   Promise   Passion   Vision   Purpose*

- Ask God to reveal to you His promise for each word He highlights to you. You may want to look up scriptures pertaining to the word highlighted.

- Write the promise down and give thanks for it. For example: "Abide in Me that your joy may be full," "I am the God who heals you," or "Your love for me is endless and beyond measure." Put these promises in a place you will see daily, repeating them over and over until they become a permanent promise in your soul.

- Read Romans 12:6–8, 1 Corinthians 12:8–10, and 1 Peter 4:11.

- Make a list of the spiritual gifts and note the gift God is highlighting to you. Ask God for the gift you are longing for.

- Allow Him to show you what He is doing right now. Envision yourself partnering with Him as you use this gift to bring heaven to earth.

- Activate your gift this week by stepping out in faith to use it.

- Continue this exercise, practicing the gift daily as if it were fully activated. Don't be afraid of failure; just keep stepping out.

- Keep a journal of what God is doing to build your faith.

> *"And I pray that he would unveil within you the unlimited riches of his glory and favor until supernatural strength floods your innermost being with his divine might and explosive power."*
> Ephesians 3:16

_____

_____

_____

_____

_____

_____

_____

_____

# CONCLUSION: INTO JOY

Looking back over the journey, I see an affectionate, devoted Father bringing His beloved daughter into a close companionship with Him. In His presence, I found myself captivated by His majesty and passionate love for me. Learning to change the way I think revealed that my life is about the journey, a journey where I am loved and cherished by a faithful Father. He woos me into His arms daily, bringing healing and restoration to my heart and salvation that is forming me into His image. It is in this place of sweet intimacy I find joy, His exuberant joy. Joy that gives me strength, courage, and peace; joy that produces an intense passion for more of Him; joy that causes me to love whom He loves and to desire to go where He is going. Through this desire, everyone in my realm of influence will have an opportunity to know His glorious love, His passionate nature, and His unblemished character.

The encounters I have with Jesus must result in a transformation every time, a renewed heart, a refinement of lifestyle. They are a challenge to receive more of His love and to love others well. Keeping one foot firmly planted on the ground and still getting the benefits of swimming in the river of God is not an option. I must let go of all control and jump in the river with Him, trusting all of Him with all of me. I experience an all-consuming love from Jesus while in His presence, filling me with His joy, compelling me closer and closer to Him.

I pray that as you journeyed with me through these visions, joy has filled your soul in a deeper loving relationship with your heavenly Father. I bless you to dream big, strengthening yourself in His joy all along the path. When the Holy Spirit reveals Jesus to us and we hear His voice, our lives change beyond anything we can think or imagine, giving the world around us a taste of heaven.

- Take time to look over your journey throughout this book. Focus on the beauty and treasure you have received, the unlimited riches of God.
- Ask the Holy Spirit to reveal to you a next step in your life. What has the Lord set you free to do? Who has He set you free to be?
- Using your path or writing in your journal, create a statement of who you are in Christ and the unlimited riches of His glory that you have inherited.

*"These things I have spoken to you, that My joy may remain in you, and that your joy may be full."*
*John 15:11 NKJV*

## Small Group Leaders Guide

A.  Leader Prep: If possible, as a leader work through the entire book before planning to lead a small group. While leading, rework the chapter you are leading with your group. Spend time each week praying for every person in your group by name.

B.  Spend time in prayer asking the Lord for what He wants to do in this small group. Write out a vision statement for the time you will be together. Share together as a group on each meeting day in the form of a declaration.

**Possible Examples:**
- I am listening and expecting to hear from God in new and refreshing ways.
- I am stepping into freedom from stuck places in my life through new revelations from God.
- Through the Holy Spirit's inspiration, I will create something that will bring life and freedom to others in my group.
- As I am set free from lies I have been believing, I will be activated in spiritual gifts in a new way so I can partner with God in ministering to others.

C.  Formulate a plan for your meeting including how you will spend your time, what you want to include, and how many weeks you will meet.

**Possible Plan:**
- Class will meet together for eight weeks
- If group is larger than eight, then find space for people to sit in groups of 6–8 for sharing and ministering to one another
- Class will go for an hour and a half:
    - Welcome/worship: 30 minutes
    - Leader time: 10–20 minutes
    - Individual activation: 20 minutes
    - Sharing and ministering: 20 minutes

D.  Teaching Format: Lead from your own gifting, making sure those in your group have space to work from their gifting.

**Possible format for week 1:**

1. Welcome statement: "For the next eight weeks we will be on a journey with Jesus. Our goal is simply to go deeper into His heart of love and hear from Him in a new way, bringing freedom to our lives. The chapters are short, and I encourage you to read the chapter discussed in group and do all the activations during the week. One of the most important parts of this group time will be sharing with one another what we hear from the Lord. Even if what we hear seems insignificant to us, we must risk sharing, for it may bring freedom and hope to someone in our group. During my preparation for this class, I sensed the Lord wanting to . . . . Each week we will begin our time declaring the work of the Lord over us."

2. Introduction
   - Have each person introduce themselves by stating an area they would like freedom from in their life (fear, anxiety, etc.)
   - Have each person share where they are in their current faith journey (stuck, intimate joy, wanting more, refreshed, etc.)

3. Leading: Read 1 Corinthians 1:10
   - Ask the following questions:
     - What does unity mean to you?
     - What is your experience with unity? (This could be open to the church, politics, cultures, racism, family issues.)
     - Do you ever feel you are always right and everyone else is wrong? Describe one time you felt this way.
   - Share a short intro to the vision. As the leader you can share your own thoughts or use some ideas from Linda's introduction.
   - Read the vision. Invite everyone to close their eyes as you read if they choose. Practice this so you can read with passion, as if you were experiencing it for the first time.

4. Activation
   - Turn on worship music and pray, "Holy Spirit, we invite You into this place. We repent for choosing to wear our own coats of life experiences without turning them over to You. We want an answer to the question 'how do I love well?' Speak to each one of us now as only You can. Soften our hearts to the love of Jesus."
   - Walk them through activation 1 in the book. You may want to choose one or two of the steps depending on your time.

5. Sharing: Invite people to share with their small groups what they have heard.

6. Closing: Invite each person to pray with the person next to them, speaking words of encouragement and life as led by the Holy Spirit.

7. Homework: Encourage everyone to read the first chapter and continue to walk through all the activations, allowing God to continue to speak into their hearts. Come back next week ready to share God-given revelations.

**Possible format for weeks 2–7:**

1. Worship

2. Group sharing: Spend ten minutes allowing each group member to share what they heard from the Lord during the week as they completed the activations, sharing any creative work they completed during the week.

3. Teaching: Introduce the new chapter and read through the vision.

4. Activation: Talk through activation 1, choosing one or two steps depending on your time.

5. Sharing: Invite people to share with their small groups what they have heard.

6. Closing: Invite each person to pray with the person next to them, speaking words of encouragement and life as led by the Holy Spirit.

7. Homework: Encourage everyone to read the current chapter and continue to walk through all the activations, allowing God to continue to speak into their hearts. Come back next week ready to share God-given revelations. (On week 7 encourage the class to complete the activations from the conclusion as well.)

**Possible format for week 8:**

1. Worship

2. Testimonies: Spend the entire time sharing testimonies of breakthrough, allowing time for those with testimonies to pray over the group for more breakthrough in those specific areas.

3. Declaration: Have everyone write out a declaration over their life that will position them to continue to move forward. Allow each person to share their declaration with their small group.

4. Encourage each person to find another group of 6–8 to lead through the book.

5. Close in prayer, rejoicing over the work of the Lord.

*Join other women on the Journey.*

**Has this book had an impact on you?**
Share your story and activation creations with Linda Withers and other women by e-mailing mystory@pathwayinsights.com.

**Want to stay connected?**
Sign up for free e-mail updates at pathwayinsights.com. You can also find us on social media and join the online community.

Learn more about Linda Withers, Pathway Insights, and speaking events at pathwayinsights.com. To inquire about inviting Linda to speak, e-mail stephanie@pathwayinsights.com.